An extraordinary journey through a
turbulent Queensland childhood

THE BIG PEOPLE'S GAME

ISAAC CURGENVEN

Published in Australia by Isaac Curgenven

First published in Australia 2024
This edition published 2024
Copyright © Isaac Curgenven 2024
Typesetting: WorkingType (www.workingtype.com.au)
Cover Design: WorkingType Design

The right of Isaac Curgenven to be identified as the
Author of the Work has been asserted in accordance with the
Copyright, Designs and Patents Act 1988.

All rights reserved. No part of this publication may be reproduced, stored in a retrieval system, or transmitted, in any form or by any means without the prior written permission of the publisher, nor be otherwise circulated in any form of binding or cover other than that in which it is published and without a similar condition being imposed on the subsequent purchaser.

 A catalogue record for this book is available from the National Library of Australia

ISBN Paperback 978-0-6486224-2-0
ISBN Ebook ?

Contents

Preface	1
Introduction	3
Albany	5
Burleigh Heads	13
Graceville	31
East Brisbane	43
Robertson	52
Sunnybank and Sunnybank Hills	59
MacGregor	69
Main Beach	85
Runcorn	93
Woodridge	106
Runcorn part Deux (like Hot Shots!)	112
Hillcrest	125
The Wedding	131
Saying Goodbye.	140
Dear Kids,	148
Author bio:	154

Preface

I dedicate this book to my children and family, hoping to explain who I was, who I am, and who I strive to be. Your loving father, husband, friend and Bruh (as my kids call me). I am sharing these memories and moments with you to provide an insight into my early life and what it has taken to get where we are. As I write, Dirty Honey's "Scars" plays in the background, helping me process the emotions that simmer just beneath the surface. There are countless triggers, but I am working through them, getting to know my skeletons one by one, and ultimately letting them go.

My purpose for this book is twofold. One; to be a catalyst for change and acknowledge that sharing our personal journeys is hard, however may help others navigate through life when we feel like there is no roadmap. Secondly and equally as important; use it as a tool to break down stigma and silence around domestic and family violence.

I don't believe I'm special. I am just someone who found their voice and has a platform to speak up. I have found that sharing our stories helps us connect on a deeper level. My hope is that by reading this book, it will help you find the strength to face your own battles and the courage to share your own story one day.

Together, we can make the world a safer and more compassionate place for everyone.

Introduction

Defining Moment – 2002

Night is falling, and here I stand on the overpass linking Sunnybank Plaza to Sunny Park Shopping Centre, weighing up my life and where to go from here. I feel so alone, unwanted, and unloved. Everyone I know or grew up with has left, each with their own reasons but with the common thread being self-preservation. I get it, but that doesn't make it any easier.

If I jump, I wonder if the fall would kill me. It doesn't look high enough, so I inspect the blue, metal spiked guardrail separating the east and westbound traffic. It feels like a painful way to go, getting impaled on a fence. Maybe if I land in front of a truck, it'll provide a backup plan - if the fall doesn't do the job, the semi will.

But how messed up would that be for the driver or whoever finds me? Why pass my baggage onto them?

Then it dawns on me; ending it here proves him right.

Fuck that.

This was a defining moment in my young life. It was when I drew my line in the sand. I would never stand in another man's shadow or let that darkness win. It's moments like these, raw and painful, that shaped who I am. I've faced countless battles before and after this moment, each one carving a piece of my story, and many depicted in the tattoos etched onto my skin.

This book is a deeply personal reflection of my life and my reality. While all the names have been changed to protect the identities of those involved, the experiences and emotions shared within these pages are authentically mine. I have written this story with a spirit of healing, love, and learning, aiming to provide a truthful recount of my journey as seen through my own eyes.

Telling this story has been challenging, especially in balancing my narrative with the privacy of others. To navigate this delicate task, I sought feedback from the handful of people who remain in contact with me and who are part of what I call my "past life." Their input has been invaluable in ensuring this account remains accurate, respectful, and considerate.

As Professor Bruttenholm in Hellboy (2004) wisely said, "In the absence of light, darkness prevails." I don't always take my life philosophy from movies but in this case its correct. Besides, who doesn't love a good hero revenge flick?

Albany

I was born in Albany, Western Australia, in the winter of 1983 to a beautiful single mum. She was tiny; only 5'3 with a slender frame, shoulder-length dark hair, and big brown eyes. My mum was what they called back in the day a hippie and a throwback to seventies culture bursting with creativity, thanks to her artistic upbringing. Mum was in her early twenties when she had me, and back then, being a single mother was heavily frowned upon. People thought she was throwing away her life by bringing a child into the world this way, and they openly questioned if she should have gone through with the pregnancy. I was told it was Pop who really supported her through the process, so thanks for sticking it out, Mum.

Apparently, I was a bit "funny looking" at birth. I had this long neck, and when they placed me on Mum's chest, I lifted my head and looked around. They reckoned I looked like something out of "The Triffids." Originally, I was named Luke, but Mum changed to Isaac before we left the hospital. Isaac Michael Curgenven. Michael, or Mick, was my uncle's name. He was a budding musician and guitarist who had tragically taken his own life a few years earlier. Bonnie Tyler's 'Total Eclipse of the Heart' was number one in the Aussie charts when I arrived. Not many people remember songs when they are newborns and I am no different, but what a banger to come out to. I will sprinkle songs of significance through this telling of my story to help define the period of each chapter and to help make an awesome playlist! Isaac, for the record, means 'the bringer of laughter' so hopefully that holds true as you read through some of these stories.

I was conceived in Brisbane, but mum went back to Western Australia once pregnant to give birth. I am not sure why. There was no father's name on my birth certificate and growing up, I was told my dad was an Italian surfer dude with the last name 'Stone' who wasn't ready to be a father. Later DNA results suggest he was more likely Norwegian or Iberian. I'm not sure why they didn't stay together or if he even knew Mum was pregnant. I've come to terms with the fact I might never know.

People sometimes ask if I want to find him.

It's difficult to pinpoint how I feel about him. Part of me wonders if he even knew I was born, if he ever asked for a photo, or if he ever wanted to meet me. I wonder if he would have been more loving than the stepfathers I had, or how my life might have turned out differently if Mum and he had stayed together. Meeting him now would likely be a mix of disappointment - whether it would be a shock to realise, "Damn, I come from that guy?!" - or a sense of awe, thinking, "What a great bloke and where were you for those 20 years I needed you?"

There's also a part of me that hopes meeting him might provide some closure, helping to fill in the blanks of my family history and offering insight into any health or medical issues that might affect my own children. Not to mention the family tree question. Do I have any brothers or sisters out there? Do they look like me? I suspect the truth about him is somewhere in the middle as neither the hero nor the villain, but a complex figure who, like all of us, had his own share of imperfections and potential. Ultimately, the quest for understanding my biological father would not be just about seeking answers, but also about reconciling with the past and making sense of how it has shaped who I am today.

And let's not forget, there are a LOT of missed Christmas and birthday presents outstanding.

My first home was the small town of Albany about five hours south of the capital Perth, where I lived with my mum and her parents in an old weatherboard home near the ocean. Nan was a larger lady, with grey curly hair and a big smile. She was an amazing artist, and her beautiful paintings adorned our walls. Pop was a World War II veteran who worked for Telecom and on the rail lines in regional Western Australia. Apparently, my first word was "ARNA," which is what I called my beloved nan.

We lived together for the first twelve to eighteen months of my life. Being a single mum in the early '80s at the young age of twenty-three would have come with immense pressure to put me up for adoption, but with her parents' support, she made it through this challenging period. Nan had two kids from her previous marriage and another three with Pop—two boys and three girls – five kids in total, so they knew a thing or two about parental pressures and small-town gossip. Both grandparents and Mum's younger sister were there when I was born in the Royal Albany Hospital, and between the four of them, I received my first of many cuddles.

Nan and Pop were incredibly loving and doting. Being the first grandson and the first to carry the Curgenven name, I held a special place in their hearts. They showered me with affection and attention, filling my childhood with wonderful memories. There are pictures of stroller rides, building sandcastles, cozy cuddles, road trips, and learning to walk. My earliest memories are filled with the warmth of her love and the security of Pop's strong, reassuring presence. While my pop was a man of few words, I was happy to simply sit on his lap and watch TV. His calm demeanour evened out Nan's creative buzz.

I'd spend time in the garden helping Nan, surrounded by the vibrant colours of her flowers and the soothing sounds of nature. Her garden was a wonderland. She had a knack for growing the most beautiful flowers that she would prune, pick and arrange to paint in these beautiful bouquets. I would toddle around, fascinated by the buzzing bees and fluttering butterflies. Pop would join us; his rough hands gentle as he showed me how to plant seeds and water the plants. These moments were more than just play. They were lessons in patience, care, and the beauty of nurturing life.

I have always loved animals, especially cats. Nan had a few around the house, and I would spend hours playing with them. One of my favourite photos is of me as a toddler, sitting in the garden with a cat named Sylvester after the cartoon character curled up on my lap, both of us happy and at peace.

Their home was always filled with love and creativity. Nan's art supplies were always within reach. I would watch her paint, mesmerized by the way she brought her visions to life. I would often be the focal point of her art, with amazing portraits and sketches that would be entered into local art competitions, winning many of them. She encouraged my budding artistic talents, giving me crayons and paper and praising my early scribbles as if they were masterpieces.

Nan loved retelling me the story about the time I found her false teeth under her pillow and her makeup applicator sponge on the bedside table. I ran to her in a panic, thinking I'd found her teeth and tongue! She always had a good laugh about it. She would read me Winnie the Pooh and Christopher Robin stories, her soothing voice bringing the characters to life. Those moments felt magical, a special bond that was different from the one I shared with Mum. While Mum was my rock, guiding me and keeping me safe, Nan was my haven of warmth and indulgence. She had the luxury of spoiling me without the daily worries, financial burdens, and stresses that Mum faced.

Their support extended beyond the everyday. They were my anchors; providing stability and love in a world that could often be uncertain and challenging. They stood by Mum, giving her the strength and support she needed to navigate single motherhood. Their home was a safe haven; a place where I felt loved, cherished, and protected.

At my core though, I was always a 'mamma's boy'. My mother was my best friend, my support network, and my guiding light. She did her best in those early years to play both roles, and from what I remember, I always felt safe and loved. My happy place was with my head in her lap, with her fingers running through my hair. It was the best feeling in the world. I never asked too many questions about my dad because I didn't want to upset her. Besides, in my eyes, I wasn't missing out on anything. Between the three of them, I had all the love, care and attention I could dream of. My small world felt very full.

But in 1985, we relocated to Ashgrove in Queensland, and moved in with some of Mum's friends and their two kids. One of them gave Mum a toy monkey for me, which I aptly named "Monkey." He quickly became my favourite toy and is one of the few items I still have to this day. He is a handheld puppet, so my mum would always read stories to me as monkey and then smother me in monkey kisses right before bed. It's a truly cherished core memory.

I don't know why Mum moved back to Brisbane, the other side of the country from Albany. After spending the first part of my life with my grandparents, I was uprooted from them and moved across the country with Mum to start over. The move was abrupt, and I was too young to understand the reasons behind it. Perhaps mum needed a fresh start or felt the pull of familiar surroundings? Maybe she was trying to reconnect with my dad? Whatever the reason, it marked the beginning of a transient period in our lives. Brisbane, with its humid subtropical climate and bustling city, was a stark contrast to the serene, and freezing coastal beauty of Albany.

When I was two, Mum and I moved to Cairns and Cape Tribulation for a short while. We would spend our mornings walking on the beach, collecting shells and driftwood, and building sandcastles. I loved exploring and had a great attention span for a child my age. Time seemed to slow down during those days, and I was completely content.

We moved back to Ashgrove later that year and then to Mt Gravatt in 1986.

I only recall snippets from this time in my life. Memories flash by like a montage reel. I remember being dropped at a babysitter's house and running around the fenced yard, screaming for my Mum to come back for hours on end. I don't think the sitter ever agreed to watch me after that. Instead, I was booked into daycare on level two of City Hall at King George Square. I can recall the sandpit by the window, my apparent fear of heights, the big round arched windows and the bell tower chime that would echo throughout the whole city.

I once tried to shave my legs in the bathtub after watching Mum and ended up with the razor stuck in my leg. There was blood everywhere and I nearly gave her a heart attack.

We'd have fish and chips at the Redcliffe Jetty with my mum's big sister and her three kids. I'd keep my eyes peeled for sharks after watching one of the Jaws films with Mum at the cinemas with a big box of buttered popcorn (which along with Nan's famous scones, jam and cream are my all-time favourite comfort food).

I'd hide Mum's ciggies in the back bucket seat of her old blue and white Ford. One time we were pulled over by the police for having a dashboard fan in those pre-air conditioner days.

She would teach me how to cook, although I could never master her Coconut Cream Pie. She would handmake most of my clothes. They were fun creations from second hand or left over material. Sure, the legs would be different lengths and occasionally the hole for my head would be too small, but looking back at these old and faded photos we were uniquely us.

Astro Boy and Transformers, like me, were more than meets the eye.

Despite being on opposite sides of the country, we would talk on the telephone to my grandparents every week. Our relationship was unique. There was an extra layer of tenderness and patience; a different kind of love that only grandparents can provide. They offered a sense of continuity and history, connecting me to the past while helping me navigate the present. Their love was a constant source of joy and stability in my life.

Burleigh Heads

Everything changed when my Mum met my future stepfather. He was a formidable presence; tall and intimidating, with a build reminiscent of Hulk Hogan. He had long hair with a bald patch on top and a handlebar moustache, though his hair was black, not platinum blonde. I once told him, 'You have pig skin on your head,' referring to his pink bald patch. Standing around 6'3" to 6'4" (192-195 cm) and weighing north of 100 kg, he was a man who ran daily and lifted weights afterwards. He was about 51 when he entered our lives, while Mum was just 26, meaning I would be about 3 years old. Mum and I share a birthday just one day apart, both Geminis.

My first memory of him was at Burleigh Heads. It wasn't until I found some old letters and photos that I realized he had been part of our lives for over a year earlier at Mt. Gravatt. A few clear-cut memories stand out vividly. The first was my intense dislike of him being with MY mum. I remember sneaking into their bedroom and pulling apart his neatly made bed in a futile attempt to drive him away. Instead of achieving my goal, this act of rebellion seemed only to reinforce the idea that mum couldn't manage me alone and needed him to be the disciplinarian. It only cemented his role as the enforcer in our household.

Mum obviously had strong feelings for him, but I couldn't understand why. To my young eyes, she was so pretty and delicate, and he seemed to be her polar opposite. It was always clear that he was not my father. There was never any confusion about the subject. As such, he never called me "son" and I never called him "dad." The closest we got to expressions of affection were the occasional hug and being told, "lots of love." It was a phrase that fell well short of, "I love you." I understand now that this was likely a generational norm, but still left an emotional void.

We all moved in together in a rental at Burleigh Heads on Banksia Broadway, just across from Burleigh Beach. He was working at Boggo Road Gaol and Numinbah Valley Correctional Centre, so the proximity to his work was the reason for this location. He was an authoritarian 'leader' and a strict vegetarian, long before it became trendy, and we both had to follow suit. It wasn't too hard a change, as we never ate much meat or dairy anyway. I had grown used to having my mum all to myself. Our little routines. Our quiet moments. Now, I had to share her with a stranger who was completely different to us, and our worlds collided.

I didn't want to share my mum with anyone, and I definitely DID NOT want or need a new dad. We had done fine for the first few years together, why did we need the change? From the moment he walked through the door, I felt something was off. I was too young to explain or have the words to articulate it, but something that made my stomach churn. Almost as much as my stomach churned when he would force me to smell his 'bellybutton fluff' it was like a makeshift birds nest in there or just as repulsive to bite down on bars of soap if I spoke out of turn or my tone wasn't appreciated. This was him testing her boundaries as much as I was testing his.

The more I would rebel and push back, the more the punishment or discipline would be inflicted. He had convinced mum that's what I needed since I didn't have a father figure, a strong hand, lessons from the school of hard knocks.

He could do whatever to me, as long as it was called 'tough love'.

He also dabbled in doing psychic readings. While I'm told he was not overly accurate, he was great at reading people, and would spout Oahspe and Silver Birch to single young women searching for answers and spiritual awareness. That is how we met a wonderful young woman who was in her early 20s and who soon joined the family unit as my 'auntie.' She was this bubbly, red-haired, beautiful country girl. The first thing I ever said to her was, "do you know your eyes disappear when you smile?" which is the definition of ironic for anyone who has ever seen me smile. Together with Mum, she went to work at a property promotions business at Surfers Paradise. Mum fell pregnant with my little sister in 1987 and suddenly, our home went from two to five seemingly overnight.

When Mum came home from the hospital with my little sister in early 1988, I was so happy. The family unit felt complete, and I was smitten with her. I would cuddle up next to Mum and hold her. I would just sit there in awe of this newborn beauty. Since my mum obviously trusted my stepfather and he stayed with her, unlike my birth father, I tried to fall in line for the sake of my new family.

Mum's attention, once solely focused on me, now divided among a larger family unit and understandably focused on the youngest member of our family. I navigated feelings of confusion and frustration, longing for the simplicity of times when it was just Mum and me. Each day became a barrage of new experiences and emotions as I learned to adapt to this newfound family dynamic, where moments of fun and togetherness were peppered with challenges and the need to find my place among the larger household. When it was good it was great, but when it was bad it was terrible.

Writing these memories out has me feeling oddly nostalgic. Christmas this first year together was fun. I remember when I opened my bedroom door, my Mum and Aunty had put coloured string from my door to different locations where my presents had been hidden. It was a really fun day.

Not that it would have changed anything, but I tried to give him a chance. I really did. There was always this nagging feeling in my gut, something that told me he wasn't who he made out to be; like he was playing a role, and I was the only one who saw through the act. Mum's perception of him was not my reality.

Mum was happy, or at least seemed to be. She was the cook, the cleaner, the lover and provider of the household. It was a big adjustment for us all. I told her my fears and she could see me changing under this new regime, but my concerns were downplayed time and again.

One night, I overheard them arguing. Their voices were low, but the tension was thick. He was saying things about how she needed to let go of the past and how this family was her only family.

"You are 100% in or 100% out."

"Good luck being a single mum with two kids, to two dads out there in the world."

"It's my way or the highway."

He was trying to control her, to change her, and push her for complete obedience.

I didn't have all the answers, but I knew that I had to listen to that feeling in my gut. It was the start of something new for me; learning to trust myself regardless of what the adults said. I tried to listen to that inner voice that told me when something was wrong. As much as I hated the idea of sharing Mum, I knew I had to protect her, especially if she couldn't see what I saw. I was truly scared of the man and tried to toe the line, but that feeling in the pit of my stomach never went away.

Our beautiful beach house just one street back from the iconic Burleigh Heads Beach. Every day, I rode my push bike to Burleigh Heads Primary School with my mum walking close behind. In the sandpit there, I'd dig for hours, searching for broken blue tiles that I imagined as sparkling gemstones. Looking back, they were probably covered in asbestos drywall. In the front oval, 'pinecone wars' were our favourite before school pastime, with teams strategically positioned on either side of the garden. The green pinecones were like rock missiles, capable of shredding anyone they hit, while the brown ones scattered on the ground were our readily available ammunition. Looking back now, that game was brutal! What were we thinking?

After school, it wasn't uncommon to find myself home alone, without keys to let myself in. I'd improvise by climbing over the railing onto the patio cover, and then squeezing through an open window. That same patio was my launching pad I utilised, inspired by the 1986 movie 'The Boy Who Could Fly.' I'd gather as many plastic shopping bags as I could carry, insert my arms through the handles, and leap off, hoping to soar—or at least float—like in the movies. It was a time of youthful dreams and daring escapades, where every afternoon held the promise of adventure and the chance to defy gravity, even if just for a moment.

Kindergarten and Grade One were formative years filled with mixed emotions. I was excited to start school. It was a stark contrast to my initial struggles with separation anxiety when I was first dropped at babysitters or daycare. Something had shifted within me. I felt ready to embrace the new adventure of learning and making friends. On that first day at school, I confidently chose my table and chair, turned to Mum with a smile, and said, "Well... see you later then." It marked a milestone where my growing independence met Mum's pride in seeing me take this new step with courage and enthusiasm.

As a young nipper at Burleigh Beach, I have vivid memories of Norfolk pines standing tall against the coastal breeze. The red bottlebrush flowers added splashes of vibrant colour, while the sky echoed with calls of rainbow lorikeets, their feathers painting the ground in a kaleidoscope of colours. That dried salt texture on my face and hair mixed with the soft sand between my toes was always a recipe for a great day. In the summertime, you would have to sprint on your tippy toes to save the rest of your feet from getting cooked on the hot sand.

Burleigh Beach wasn't just a place; it was my first real home in my mind. It was a playground of exploration and discovery, where every day brought new experiences and unexpected lessons that shaped my early years. Each morning was an adventure of its own as we'd combed through the rocky shoreline in search of hidden treasures and shells of all shapes and sizes. I found an incredible conus shell lodged between the rocks and needed a wrecking bar to wedge it out.

I'd search through the area, hunting for the newly minted $2 coins, which were released in 1988. They seemed to be scattered everywhere, and I became quite adept at spotting them glinting in the sunlight. When required, even venturing into stormwater drains in search of gold! I once came across a stingray that had been bitten and killed by a shark and had washed ashore. I moved its body in a plastic bag and took it to school as a very stinky show and tell.

Another time we found hundreds of bouncy balls washed up and it was weeks of fun until they were all lost. My stepfather found a duffel bag of clothes once on a morning run, which he took home, washed and then wore all the time.

Like most of my life, there were lessons learned the hard way. I quickly discovered the painful truth about bluebottle jellyfish, while they may burst when you jump on their floating top, they do not die, and those tentacles will projectile up into your leg hair and sting like crazy.

While on the topic of learning things the hard way, after not paying enough attention to house guests he had invited around, all my personal belongings took flight off the balcony onto the driveway below. On a separate occasion, my prized Donkey Kong handheld game was placed in front of me on the kitchen bench. Both my hands were held either side of the small brown game as it was viciously smashed, thirty centimetres from my face, with a sledgehammer. Button batteries, plastic and the screen shattered everywhere. It was a similar story when I was caught riding my bike without a helmet. Same idea, just using a tomato to show what happens to a human head when in contact with a car. He wasn't wrong. Maybe a little overly theatrical. The image is still etched in my mind and I always wear a helmet.

I got lost twice during my time there. The first time was in Burleigh Mall on James Street. It was a labyrinth of shops and when it was bustling with people, it was easy for a young kid to wander off and lose track of where they were. I remember the panic rising as I realized I was separated from whoever I was with. It was only a few blocks to walk home, but in these years, long before mobile phones, you were taught if you were lost, then you stay where you are and don't talk to strangers until you were found, which eventually happened, and no doubt felt longer than it *actually* was.

The other time was even more disorienting. Someone was looking after me, and rather than staying at our house, she took me to her place.

I wasn't familiar with her surroundings. I can still visualise details of the room, but when I realized I really didn't know where I was, there was another big kafuffle. Tears, confusion, and a flurry of phone calls later, I was reunited with my family, but not without a lot of worry and anxiety in between. These incidents taught me the importance of staying close, paying attention to your surroundings while on the move, and the relief of being found again. Mum would always come find me. Back then, I still believed nothing could come between us.

When mum wasn't working, we'd play tennis together and talk about our day. This became my favourite past time. Sure, there was the satisfying whack of the ball against the racket cutting through the coastal breeze, but it was the only time we had to ourselves, and the rest of the world seemed to fade away.

When I was with my mates, we'd play footy and try to emulate our favourite players. The mighty Penrith Panthers led by Greg Alexander and the newly formed Brisbane Broncos with Alfie Langer and his darting chip and chase, were my sporting heroes. The neighbourhood kids were all older than me. My stepfather saw me take a hit while playing footy the front yard. I was steamrolled but got up and kept playing without so much as a tear. Yeah, it hurt, but I didn't want to look weak in front of the guys. Unfortunately for me, that set the new minimum threshold for the type of hits I could take. That moment essentially set the precedent for years to come.

There was no place for weakness around him. I can't even say we had physical fights as that would give too much credibility to my ability to fight back. It was just a beating. Not with fists. A long handle wooden stirring spoon or leather belt was his go-to during this time but wasn't uncommon to be thrown across a room or into a wall, being held down by your head and having iced water poured over your, or the hot water cut off during a shower. Open hand hits left no bruises.

The physical stuff was over relatively quick. It was his mind games that were designed to try to run you down, drain your energy and get inside your head. They were constant.

I was almost relieved when I fell seriously ill with viral meningitis. It hit me hard enough that I ended up in the hospital. Mum rushed me to the emergency department at Gold Coast Hospital where I spent a whole week. I was too young to appreciate the danger of the condition. When the nurses tried to draw blood, my veins collapsed. They had to roll me onto my stomach and draw the samples from my back. I cried and begged them to fake the results and have been terrified of needles ever since that day.

It was during that hospital stay that I got my first, and throughout my childhood, last chance to watch The Simpsons. The TV in the hospital room offered a brief escape from the medical drama unfolding around me.

The kid in the bed next to mine had been in a car accident, and I couldn't help but notice the triangle shaped tape covering the stitches around his neck. It looked gnarly, but for a young boy it was a stark reminder of how fragile life can be and how quickly things can change. Those days in the hospital were a mix of fear, agony, and curiosity, which shaped my outlook on health and resilience.

Happy to say I made a full recovery and made it out better than the person in this next story. I had ridden down to the corner shops to get a haircut. As per usual, I was chatting away with the hairdresser. I loved having a yarn with anyone who'd listen. There was an older lady sitting next to me with a hair dryer on, and she was really quiet and unresponsive to my questions, which I found a bit rude. I asked the hairdresser what was wrong with her and she went to check. That's when we realised the poor darling had suffered a heart attack and passed away right there in the chair. The hairdresser tried to lighten the moment, joking that I must have bored her to death. I was completely freaked out! I kept thinking the ambulance would come for her and the cops for me. I half-expected to see the whole thing on the 6pm news, but it never made it.

That day stuck with me for a long time. It was my first brush with death, and it left me feeling uneasy. I couldn't go back to that shop again for fear of the repercussions of what I did to that poor old lady.

In letters written to me years later, Mum explained she needed help with disciplining me. That responsibility fell on my stepfather, with little oversight or interference. It was 'for my own good'. I'm not sure how naughty a 4-year-old can be, but now having three kids of my own, I understand the phases: 'the terrible twos, the forgettable threes, and the f-ing fours'. Still, it is never necessary to resort to that type of violence and standover tactics to discipline a child. I vowed to break that cycle of trauma for my children, wife and loved ones.

He had these sweet nicknames for me like ponce, prat and little lord Fauntleroy. He must have thought I was a gay, little shit with good dress sense, I guess? He wasn't *completely* wrong… I always dress well.

He would tell us stories of his younger self growing up in Townsville with a large family of five brothers and sisters. Eventually, he had schooling down in Brisbane at Christian Brothers. He would go on and on about stories of his time in the Army Reserves, working as a carpenter (and would jokingly compare himself to Jesus, but that's about where the similarities ended) and tales of missed opportunities buying land where the Carindale shopping centre was eventually built and close calls with gangs in Fortitude Valley back in the 60's. He often said his instincts kept him alive and warned me to always be aware of my surroundings and keep my head on a swivel. Ironically, he would always tell us to trust your gut feeling, just not with him. To my knowledge, we never actually met any of his family but were introduced to several 'brothers' who were of no direct relation.

Looking back on these stories now, it's hard to know what was real and what was embellished, especially as his beliefs in spirituality deepened. He started preaching to us about concepts like 'mind over matter' and what your mind can conceive, your body can achieve. He talked about unlocking the human mind to achieve extraordinary feats, like enhanced regeneration, past life regression, levitation, and the ability to choose one's own sexuality or materialise health and wealth. It was always foretold that my mum and I had multiple past lives together in different relationship dynamics dating back to ancient Egypt (if you believe that stuff). It may help explain in part our complicated relationship as I grew up. These notions seemed fantastical and surreal to my adult self, yet they were a central part of his worldview during that time and were enforced on us. As a family we would watch Robert Stack and Unsolved Mysteries that would seemingly support some of these theories. I would go the extra mile and collect 'The Unexplained, Mysteries of Mind, Space and Time' magazines that were released monthly from our local newsagency for .99 cents. I would lean into these wonderful ideas trying to find a sense of belonging or acceptance.

On the long drives between the Gold Coast and Brisbane, the Strawberry Farm was a cherished stop on every road trip. Long before the highway upgrade, which did *eventually* happen, there was a gravel exit straight to the farm. They served the most incredible homemade strawberry ice cream you could imagine for just $2.50. I carried this tradition into my adult life, often stopping there when I was working on the road. Sadly, like many good things from my past, the Strawberry Farm is no more.

We would drive to Brisbane to visit my stepfather's two older kids from a previous marriage. They lived on Brisbane's southside in Mansfield. His ex-wife once told my mum something along the lines of 'he has ruined me and I will never trust again'. This ominous warning was seemingly ignored. I guess jilted exes say the darndest things? Despite this, we would generally all visit together as a family, while on other occasions I would be dropped off for the day. Among the four of us 'kids', I was the only one who wasn't his biological child. His firstborn, my older stepsister, who was over 10 years my senior, had a rad collection of 80s cassette tapes that I loved listening to. It felt like she took a shine to me. I remember our drives together and hanging out in her room, where she'd playfully tease me with tales of Casper the friendly ghost living in her closet and Rewrite song lyrics to crack me up, the one etched in my memory was 'Isaac in the middle of the street' based on the Madness's song 'Our House'. Those times were special and made me feel a part of her world, despite our different family dynamics.

My stepbrother was different. He was always friendly but awkward around me, as I can remember. He was huge; north of two meters tall (6'10 in imperial measurements) and like his dad, built like a brick outhouse. I remember being guided into his makeshift bedroom in the bottom level garage of their 1970s two story brick family home. A giant black flag on the wall was covering the windows. I think it was Metallica. There was a sword above his bed. It was in that room that he molested me. Many of the details in my mind have been blocked out and are sketchy. I would have been only five, maybe six at the time, but I recall snippets from the interaction which I won't detail here.

Needless to say, the experience left me shaken. I was scared of being alone and developed a deep distrust of older men. I was very young and had been forced to interact with a naked, grown man. Mum realised something had happened when I asked questions about it. My language and demeanour had changed significantly and she must have told my stepfather as he acknowledged it, but it was never spoken of again. In 1990, my stepbrother ended up going away to Arthur Gorrie Correctional Centre and I never saw him much after that.

Looking back now, I don't have hate in my heart toward him for this. He was a product of his upbringing, which from second hand stories was no walk in the park either. It happened. I can't change that.

Our two-storey home in Burleigh was a similar design to their place in Mansfield, but with more of a coastal-style suited to beach living. The layout was familiar: bedrooms and kitchen upstairs, with the bathroom, office, and garage downstairs. From that day on, I developed PTSD about being alone downstairs. Whenever I needed to use the bathroom, I would quickly dash back upstairs without always remembering to flush. The fear of making noise and drawing attention to my presence downstairs was intense. My anxiety was off the charts. It was my way of trying to stay unnoticed, even in the familiarity of my own home. In my mind, it was my stepfather's son who had abused me and a part of me was expecting him to do the same. I was genuinely fearing for my safety.

My non-compliance to flushing the toilet angered him greatly. To teach me a lesson, he caught me before I could flee upstairs to the safety of my room and proceeded to flip me upside down, holding me headfirst in the toilet and flushing on me several times. Choking on the water, I had never felt so scared, helpless, and embarrassed as I did in that moment. He left me dripping wet, gasping for air and covered in my own shit, then yelled at me while forcing me to look in the mirror.

To protect myself, I would never turn my back on the bathroom door, to the point that I would sit to pee with my feet wedged against the back of the door so I would never be caught off guard again. It would take me over 20 years before re-training myself to stand up and use an open urinal. We were never permitted to lock the doors to our bedrooms, shower, toilet or anywhere. He always wanted full and unfiltered access to us at all times, and this was as close to privacy as I could secure.

After the incident with the flushing, I was strictly forbidden from venturing downstairs unless there was an emergency, like the house being on fire. It became a rule etched in stone, and for a young kid, it felt like a lifetime sentence of confinement to the upper floor. Fate, of course, tested this rule. Every Sunday without fail, I would tune in to RAGE on the ABC. It was a ritual I cherished, sitting in front of the TV, eagerly awaiting the latest music videos and trying my best to sing along to Billy Joel's "We Didn't Start the Fire." I smelled something burning and rushed into the kitchen to find smoke billowing from the stove. My heart raced with fear as I ran downstairs, burst into my stepfather's office and yelled, "THE HOUSE IS ON FIRE!" Relief washed over me when Mum quickly assured me it was just a bit of smoke from an unattended meal she was preparing, but in that moment of adrenaline and panic, I hadn't known if I was about to face a real emergency or not. I felt like I had saved the day, even if it was just a false alarm and I just hoped it would keep me in his good graces long enough to not be punished as badly the next time I stuffed up.

My grandparents made the big move from Albany to Brisbane to be closer to us, settling in Burpengary at a retirement village called 'Burpengary Pines'. It was a good 90-minute drive north, but compared to the other side of the country, it felt like they were practically next door. Whenever Mum and I drove up there, crossing over the old Gateway toll bridge used to freak me out. It seemed so steep and intimidating. I'd sit there, holding my breath, half-convinced the car would fail and start rolling backward. The view from the top was breathtaking, but the climb itself always gave me butterflies.

We had a housewarming lunch with my mum and her sisters along with Nan and Pop up at their new place. There were so many of us we couldn't all fit around the kitchen table, so we set up outside in the carport to ensure everyone had a seat. The insects in a Queensland summer are much more prevalent than they were in Albany and towards the end of lunch, this massive cockroach started climbing across the tin carport roof. We laughed when we saw it and joked it better not land on us, before it flew right at nan, landing smack bang in her plate of lunch. She screamed and jumped back, almost falling out of her chair. We all broke out in fits of laughter; even Nan, after the shock had worn off.

I know I've mentioned it already, but I can't understate how bloody amazing of an artist my nan was. She could wield any medium on a canvas: watercolour, oil, acrylic, charcoal or sketches. You name it, she nailed it. She even had her own gallery at Expo 88 in South Brisbane, now Southbank Parklands. I would help her and Pop carefully wrap each of her artworks in towels and blankets to protect the frames during transit in the boot of their car. I still remember the day we hopped on the train to see her exhibition there. It was a big deal, and she was absolutely buzzing with pride. So was I.

My grandparents' decision to move closer to us in Burpengary wasn't just about geography; they were street smart and wise to some of the happenings going on at home. They were driven by deep concerns for their daughter and grandchildren. Nan and Pop sensed something wasn't right with Mum's situation, especially with my stepfather.

They didn't get along with him, and the signs of isolation, control, and possible abuse were becoming increasingly apparent. From their perspective, being nearby meant they could keep a closer eye on us, offering support and an escape if needed. They worried about Mum's well-being and our upbringing in an environment that seemed to grow more restrictive and unsettling over time. Their move wasn't just a relocation; it was a protective measure, a way to be actively involved in our lives and to provide a buffer against any potential harm that Mum might be experiencing.

I will never forget the day my grandmother, then in her mid-60s, did something that left a lasting impression on me. Fuelled by a mixture of determination and liquid courage, she made pop drive her down to the Gold Coast with a singular purpose: to reclaim artwork that my stepfather wouldn't return. But it wasn't just about retrieving her paintings—it was about reclaiming her family.

I had always remembered her as the warm, gentle Nan who would read to me and fill the house with the scent of lavender. That day, she was like I had never seen before. She was angry and loud and drunk. The scene unfolded quickly and violently. My stepfather overpowered her, throwing her to the ground and pinning her to the floor by her face. Mum was ordered to call the police to remove her from the property. In the chaos, I was ushered away by my 'aunty', and I was thankful to be spared from witnessing the full extent of the confrontation. I still have a vivid image of Nan's anguished eyes as she screamed on the floor as I was dragged away.

I didn't know the full extent of Nan's history, as it was long before my time, but I later learned that she had struggled with alcohol and depression. Afterwards, Mum shared stories of Nan's bouts of overindulgence and her attempts to take her own life during Mum's teenage years. The children would often have to pull her out and revive her. Nan could be harsh, hurtful, and physical, and she was a force to be reckoned with. Her size alone often intimidated Pop and her kids. These were things I only heard about later; they were second-hand accounts and painted a picture of a tumultuous past that I had never witnessed firsthand, until that moment.

Nan had seen through the facade of my stepfather's spiritual "awakening" and the controlling dynamics within our family. She knew that her artworks, displayed or stored wherever they were, symbolized more than just her artistic expression. They were a part of her identity and her legacy. They represented a connection to her family, to us, that she feared might be slipping away under his influence.

Her courageous act that day wasn't just defiance; it was a statement of love and protection. By reclaiming her paintings, she was asserting her role as a guardian of family ties and a staunch defender against any attempts to diminish her influence or erase her presence from our lives. It was a powerful reminder of her strength and determination to safeguard what mattered most—her family's well-being and unity. She wanted more than the paintings back. She wanted us.

Unfortunately, as had become the norm, the actions only added fuel to the fire with my stepfather preaching he was justified in retaliating. He said Mum needed to let go of the past, that his family was her only family, and she must commit to being 100% in.

Nan and pop never visited us at home ever again.

Graceville

After a chaotic few years trying to settle into this so-called 'one big happy family,' the five of us packed up and moved to Brisbane. Why we ended up at Strong Avenue, Graceville, no one seems to remember. I started at Graceville Primary, and let me tell you, it was a real struggle to fit in and figure myself out. All these new kids, classrooms, and teachers. It was a huge adjustment. To avoid it I'd hide in the bushes—African Plumes, I think, with these bright orange flowers—to eat my lunch. There were some really cool hidden trails to explore, so I lost myself in those instead of my schoolwork. Art and doodling took over, and I started falling behind in class and hanging out with the wrong crowd.

Then, in November 1991, my pop suddenly passed away. We were lucky enough to have had an early Christmas catch-up with him. There was no sign of his impending end, but in late October, Mum had an inkling, and our stepfather allowed us to visit for the day. This turned out to be the final time we'd ever see him.

Pop was born and raised in Mount Lawley, Western Australia, growing up in the gold fields. He was a gentle soul; skinny and short man an olive complexion and a radiant smile that I inherited. He was bald from his early twenties (which I fear I may have also inherited) and wore a toupée to hide it. He always dressed neatly in a polo shirt tucked into his King Gee shorts. He was a quiet bloke who loved his VB stubbies and Winfield cigarettes. We shared simple pleasures like going to the pub or track to watch the horse races.

I would sit on his knee cheerfully counting out his loose change from a glass mason jar, which became my pocket money and laugh watching old re-runs of Get Smart.

Despite his military service, Pop never spoke much about his experiences in the war. I understand now why veterans often remain silent. I once did a primary school assignment on World War II, focusing on Pop's role as a signaller. The original photos I used were never returned. I wish I had the foresight to have made copies. My stepfather always downplayed Pop's involvement. However, as I grew older, I researched his service. The stories and records blew me away, but I'll get to that later.

Pop was my idol, and he treated me as an equal rather than a child. He was my one positive male role model growing up. We never got to say a final goodbye, and I've always felt guilty about that. Even though I know Pop's soul is still around me and we've had a few chats since, back then, it was the end of an era. The bond between a boy and his grandfather is a sacred one, and I was fortunate to share some meaningful years with my Pop. He was a constant presence in my early years and my memory of his wide grin is a testament to his joy and warmth.

My stepfather would not allow us to attend the funeral. It was a decision that left us with a deep sense of resentment for not having the chance to say goodbye properly. Pop was buried in an unmarked grave in Redcliffe, double-deep to eventually accommodate Nan, as they had planned. His sudden death at 73 left me heartbroken. It was my first family encounter with the finality of death, and I struggled to understand what happened after we die. I was told Pop believed in nothing beyond this life; that we simply live, die, and fade into the darkness.

I can only imagine the pain Nan felt discovering Pop in the bath, having succumbed to a heart attack. She moved back to Albany not long after the funeral, and I didn't see her much, though we kept in touch through letters.

There's a specific scent near their old home at Burpengary—a mix of pine, eucalyptus, and blooming flowers—that brings me a fleeting sense of Pop's presence. If I could bottle that scent, I would, as it is the closest I can get to having him here with me again. I make sure to blow him a kiss every time I pass by.

Back in the early 90s, riding your bike with a portable cassette tape player was as close to freedom as you had. The tape we were cranking while flying around on our bikes, seeing who could leave the longest skid on the footpath to Michael Jackson's 'Black or White' off the Dangerous album. A group of two or three of us would ride through the streets, hang out on the banks of the Oxley River, chase skink lizards and eat mulberries off the vine under the Walter Taylor Bridge. For years, that bike remained my trusted ally, carrying me through the ups and downs of life with a steadfastness that mirrored my own resilience. It was more than a means of transport; it was my only symbol of independence.

I was so scared of having my bike taken away from me. I rode it everywhere: to school, along the Brisbane River and through Indooroopilly shopping centre. (Does anyone remember the giant rocket ship climbing frame and slide that use to sit on the playground opposite?) It became my escape from the stresses and pressures of life and my only reliable companion through my formative years. When I pedalled away, the worries of home and school would fade into the background. The wind in my face and the rhythm of the wheels on the pavement offered a sense of liberation that was hard to find elsewhere. It wasn't just about getting from place to place; it was about reclaiming control over my own path, finding moments of peace and clarity amidst the chaos of home.

Feeling lonely and overlooked, I started to steal to get attention and make friends. Looking back, it was a way to cope with the upheaval in my life. I graduated from nicking little things from the servo to stealing loose change from my stepfather's cash drawer, and eventually notes from his wallet. I'd use the money to buy food for kids at school, trying to buy friendships. But when I got caught, and I nearly always got caught, I copped a hiding.

The pinnacle of my escapades came when I stole a new bike from a local bike shop. I got a ride home in the back of a police car with my 'wingman'. This was early in grade three, so I would have been about eight years old. My 'teenage' rebellion happened early, and a few years ahead of schedule.

I can't remember exactly what I'd done at school to warrant punishment, but I think it involved sliding down the stairway railing; a stunt I had seen on an episode of Teenage Mutant Ninja Turtles. Regardless of the reason, my grade three teacher sent me to get the cane. My scheming brain went into overdrive, and I decided to avoid the punishment by pressing my hands on the old metal port racks until I had a solid red-purple line across both palms from the heat and pressure. I went back to my classroom, sniffling and pretending to cry, telling the teacher how bad it hurt. I was promptly sent home, feeling on top of the world for getting away with it. After all, I had enough punishment going on at home, I didn't want to put up with that crap at school, too! The only issue I didn't foresee was that teachers talk, and my deception was found out quick smart. In short, they suggested Mum looked for other schooling options for me.

Obviously, with action came reaction, and my stepfather's solution to this was something he called 'the Big People's Game.' It wasn't a fun game; it wasn't a game at all. It was essentially a free pass for him to treat me like an adult and make me face the physical consequences for my actions.

His device of choice was called the Black Hand, a leather jockey whip like the ones you see in horse racing. It left welts that stung for days on your thighs, backside or open palms. Other aspects of his discipline included throwing me in the pool as a 'wake up' and throwing all my possessions into the wheelie bin. I didn't have many belongings, but my monkey, a hand-sized conus shell from Burleigh exploring, crystals from the farm one of my aunties had gifted to me, and my TinTin books were my prized possessions. I would have chased the dump truck to the tip if it meant getting those back. Fortunately, I wasn't too precious, so I jumped into the bin with old smelly food and sifted through the occasional maggots and bin juice to retrieve my essentials. The books didn't make it, but I still have monkey, a handful of crystals and my shell to this day.

Every time I got punished, it reinforced my sense of isolation. My stepfather's harsh methods made me feel like I had to fend for myself and like I couldn't rely on anyone else. Mum tried to verbally intervene sometimes, but her hands were tied, and I could see the guilt eating away at her. She couldn't physically get between us without taking serious damage. The more I got into trouble, the more I withdrew into my own world, finding solace in my art and the few treasures I managed to save from the bin.

Looking back, those early years of rebellion and punishment shaped who I became. At the time, I didn't know how to handle the loss of Poppy, so I acted out. Despite the trouble I got into, part of me felt a strange sense of accomplishment, like I was proving to myself that I could survive on my own. But deep down, I knew I was just a kid trying to navigate a world that seemed increasingly unfair and unpredictable. It taught me to trust my instincts and to hold onto the things that mattered, no matter what. Though my stepfather's 'Big People's Game' was meant to break me, it only made me more determined. Now, when I take my daughter to the beach and sift through the sand searching for shells, I'm reminded of how far I've come and the battles I've fought to be who I am today.

Our family holidays were generally *unusual*, to say the least. My stepfather had a particular fondness or gravitation towards nudist retreats, which made for some extremely awkward experiences. It's one thing to be nude in your own home, but it's entirely different to be forced that way in a communal area. On the car rides there, the B52's 'Love Shack' would play and almost felt like art imitating life. I don't think we had a single holiday that didn't blow up into a disaster at some point and end with us coming home early.

I can recall one trip from around this period we met a younger bloke who was not quite as young as mum, but definitely younger than my stepfather. He gravitated towards us, joining us in playing sports. For a brief moment, it felt like we had a normal (albeit nude) family interaction. My stepfather didn't take kindly to this guy's friendliness or intrusion. After a tense confrontation, we packed up and headed home.

Another holiday was a farm stay of sorts. I was playing on a tyre swing when my stepfather found some fresh cow manure and decided to use me for target practice. He hurled the muck at me, laughing as I tried to dodge the hits from mid-air on this swing. It was humiliating and gross, but he seemed to find it hilarious.

Holidays were *supposed* to be escapes, chances to relax and bond as a family. Instead, they were ruined by tension, confrontations, and bizarre antics, forcing us into uncomfortable situations that felt more like punishments than holidays. I often wondered why Mum went along with it all, but I guess she was trying to hold our fragile family together in any way she could.

Every trip seemed to reinforce my belief that something was really wrong with our family dynamic. While other kids came back from holidays with stories of beach adventures and theme parks, I returned with tales of shit fights (both literally and figuratively) and early departures. These experiences, while strange and often unpleasant, added to the rich and chaotic tapestry of my childhood. They taught me to find humour in the absurd, to laugh at myself and maintain resilience in the face of constant instability.

Speaking of instability, imagine being between grades three and four and your name is legally changed to fit in with the family? There were no wedding bells, they hadn't got hitched and I hadn't been formally adopted. I was simply no longer a Curgenven. A new birth certificate was issued, class photos were updated with a new name and that was that. I believe it was done to reduce questions when travelling as a party of five with three different surnames. They wanted to give off those 'normal' vibes, I guess. It was reiterated time and again that, just like my grandfather, the Curgenven name was weak.

I'm sure mum sat me down and tried to explain the practical reasons, but I couldn't shake the feeling that it was more about control and about shaping me into what they wanted. My stepfather's disdain for the Curgenven name was clear and not fitting for the 'strong family unit' he envisioned. We only were allowed to do what was good for his family. The Family.

To be clear, this is not to be confused with the 1960s cult also referred to as 'The Family.' Our group was also called, 'the family'. We all had the same last names, and those who didn't were called 'aunties', 'uncles', or 'brothers', all based around spirituality, philosophical concepts about life and reincarnation, with an undertone of sex, manipulation, and control.

The name change felt like another piece of my identity being stripped away. It was as if my past and all its connections were being erased. It was a strange feeling, looking at my new birth certificate. It was just a piece of paper, but it symbolised so much more. I felt disconnected from my roots, from Pop and the Curgenven legacy. The name didn't feel like mine. It felt like something imposed on me and another attempt to mould me into a different person. Every time I wrote it down, it was a reminder of how much my life was in constant change. I had no idea how to explain it to kids at school, so I just told them I was adopted.

Even as a kid, I recognised the irony. They wanted to project normalcy, to appear as a cohesive family unit, but our reality was anything but normal. The forced smiles, the name changes, the attempts to fit a mould we never belonged to—it was all a facade. Deep down, I knew that no amount of name changes or manufactured 'normal vibes' could cover up the cracks in our family. Through it all, I held onto the parts of my identity that mattered most. I might have been someone else on paper, but in my heart, I remained a Curgenven. The memories of Nan and Pop, and the resilience I had learned kept me grounded. No legal document could change who I truly was.

There was another older man hanging around at this time. He was friends with my stepfather and I was told he was his 'brother'. This dude gave me the creeps. I was told they were business partners, or so they claimed, though there was never a business I could see. It was always some get-rich-quick, multi-level marketing, networking, or positivity scheme. My stepfather openly and proudly referred to himself as a master manipulator. I couldn't understand the connection or why he was called a brother, as if it was a title like a doctor.

His presence was unnerving. He claimed to be a New Age Teacher and Philosopher of Life, but the so-called business ventures he and my stepfather were involved in never seemed to materialize into anything real. They would often travel overseas and always talking about the next big thing, but it all seemed to be smoke and mirrors. The only connection I could see between them was their unsettling interest in young ladies and girls, especially from Asia.

Mum told me years later the 'brothers' were eventually banned from Thailand.

I couldn't find common ground with the brother's new family either, which consisted of a younger Asian bride and her child to a past relationship. She couldn't speak English and was incredibly shy. It must have been a massive move and adjustment for them. Much like with my stepfather and my mum and aunties, the significant age gap never sat well with me. Despite the forced camaraderie and faux-family titles, there was a clear sense of hierarchy. The older males positioned themselves as the wise leaders, dispensing cryptic advice and making decisions that affected everyone. The younger adults seemingly lapped it up in awe of the message, but the kids, like me, were often left confused.

As I continued to grow and learn, I realised that trusting my instincts was crucial. The feelings of unease and suspicion were not just the paranoia of a young mind; they were warnings, guiding me to see the truth behind the facade. As I started to listen to them, I began to understand the importance of trusting your gut, no matter how many times people say you are wrong.

One day, I had faked being sick to score a day off from school to try and find some solitude by having the home to myself, when around lunchtime the phone rang. I answered it like normal, but the man's deep voice on the other end asked if I wanted to play a game. I said no and quickly hung up. Moments later, someone banged on the door so damn loud, I hid. Scared out of my mind, I used the phone to call for help but never found out who was at the door or why. This was years before the Wes Craven film 'Scream' came out. Similar vibes, though. I put it down to my stepfather playing a prank on me. He possibly cottoned on to the fact I wasn't sick. Afterwards, he'd jokingly offered to take me to the cat doctor to check my temperature, for those unfamiliar that is a thermometer in the bum.

The fights between him and my mum were getting worse. My favourite aunty used to try and hide us from them. She did everything, trying to shield us from the shouting and chaos. Often the arguments exploded from 0 to 100 in seconds, and the only place to take refuge was under the dining table or retreat to our rooms and listen to the chaos unfold behind our closed doors. The sound of smashing plates and screaming voices was deafening. It felt like the whole house was shaking, my little sister and I were just kids, clutching each other in fear, hoping it would all stop.

These moments of explosive anger and instability only reinforced the lessons I was learning about self-awareness. You'd never know what you would be walking into. You couldn't foresee what version of the people around you would be in order to anticipate it. Instead, I had to look out for myself, navigating each day with caution and a heightened sense of fight or flight.

I started to see the world differently. Every phone call, every knock at the door or every raised voice became a potential threat. My instincts, honed through years of living in chaos, were my only guide. They told me when to hide, when to speak up, and when to stay silent. Trusting them became second nature. It was an engrained, subconscious and automatic survival skill in a world that seemed perpetually on the brink of collapse.

We moved out from this house before the end of 1992, part way through the school year, During the move, we came home only to catch two mates breaking into our old house, rummaging through our packed boxes. They'd found our spare key hidden under a rock and were nicking whatever they saw value in. They didn't touch my true keepsakes, but took the only other thing I really cared about losing; my cassette tapes and bright yellow portable radio. Damn. Not the music. What was I supposed to do now?

I felt betrayed knowing they had riffled through my stuff. I thought they were my friends; the ones I had stolen cash and food for, but there they were, taking the one thing that gave me solace in this chaotic world. It was a harsh lesson about trust and one that stung more than any punishment my stepfather could dish out.

I realised then that trust wasn't something to be given lightly. The people I had let in and friends I thought I could count on had let me down. It was a stark reminder of how precarious my world was. I couldn't pick my family, but I could pick my friends. I would have to choose wiser next time. This betrayal also taught me something valuable. It showed me that trust had to be earned and not given lightly. Real friends wouldn't take from you; they would stand by you.

East Brisbane

Starting over: new house, new name, new school, new additions to our expanding family framework. My stepfather had set up businesses called 'The Motivators,' 'Positive Lifestyles,' and 'The Key of Life' to provide a platform for Public speaking and recruiting new members at Mind, Body and Soul exhibitions. His businesses were more like elaborate illusions that promised much but delivered little. Not sure if it was real or not, but he had a cheque signed by a legendary footy supercoach pinned to the wall and would brag that he taught the guy everything he knew. Despite the strict routines and the East Brisbane house's charm, life with my stepfather and his schemes was anything but stable.

I was actually beginning to enjoy moving house. New room. New setups. New beginnings. If I didn't like who I was or how I felt at my last school, it was a chance to re-invent myself. I would adorn my walls with posters, Nan's paintings, and my toys. Household rules were strict. Beds were to be made daily with military precision. If they were not, sheets would be stripped, and you would have to start again, failure to comply and you might come home to find your mattress gone or the bedroom door removed altogether. Rooms were to be cleaned and vacuumed weekly. While my mum would do all the cooking, my aunties would do the cleaning and I would do the dishes and laundry. It was a ritual that brought a semblance of order to my chaotic life and taught me not to do a half-assed job. Regardless of how mundane the task, going back and fixing it took more time than doing it right the first time.

We rented this grand old Queenslander on the Brisbane River on Laidlaw Parade, just down from Mowbray Park. It had a huge backyard where I would spend hours practising my Alfie Langer chip and chase moves on the tennis court. The ball bounced into the river a few times, and I'd have to hightail it to the closest spot downstream to try and fish it out. The house even had its own boat ramp and a balcony overlooking Brisbane city. This house had so much personality. Apparently, we were given the option to purchase it but my stepfather declined. It sold for $440,000 in 1991 and when it last changed hands in 2006, it sold for $3.75 million. I guess sometimes we focus so hard on achieving result of financial freedom our own way that we miss the opportunities right in front of us. Probably a great lesson for us all to learn.

From the balcony, we would observe the goings-on in the river each morning, like seeing a hot air balloon fall into the brown snake of a river and one of the private school rowing teams hitting a dead body, who had likely jumped off the Story Bridge. I would craft and throw paper aeroplanes from the deck, hoping to get them across the river to New Farm Park. None ever made it.

On the weekend, we would spend hours at Mowbray Park having picnics with my mum and the aunties, riding our bikes, playing frisbee or just laying in the grass watching the clouds in the sky, trying to make out what animal they looked like. We weren't permitted to go there too early or too late in the evening, as the bathrooms there had a weird reputation and oddly, always a long line of men.

I was enrolled at East Brisbane State School for the end of grade four and all of grade five. They had this amazing bell tower where my class made a short film once. It was a great place for me. I realised being the new kid was made a whole lot easier being good at *something* and found my niche in sports, starting with Aussie Rules Football, since the Brisbane Bears (now Lions) and the Gabba sportsgrounds were right next door. We could sneak in via the school to watch the team train.

Rugby League became my true love. I was quick on my feet and I joined the Cannon Hill Cannons football club, playing on the wing. My breakfast of champions was three wheatbix with honey and I'd love to wait until it went a little soggy before hoeing in. I got caught off guard one day. We had been feeding a neighbourhood cat and I mistook the bowl of cat food for my wheatbix. That only happened once. Never again. Lesson learnt. Always sniff test random bowls of food left on the bench.

When the school closed the oval during the Gabba stadium development, we'd look for new games to play. Red Rover. Bull Rush. Fly. With our love for footy, we started playing on the basketball courts until we realised how bad tackles hurt on bitumen. We switched to playing basketball instead, which I quickly became obsessed with.

I finally had friends I felt I could trust. We would swap basketball cards. The 1993 Upper Deck collection with the majestic photos of Michael Jordan soaring was our holy grail. We'd spend hours poring over those cards, trading our doubles and dreaming of playing at that level.

Between all the footy and basketball, my body must have been developing because I got really good at running, sprints in particular. I came first in the 100m and 200m races at the school's athletics carnival. Despite being too young to compete in districts, they put me against the upper grades, and I held my own, winning the 100m in under 15 seconds. My success in sports also helped me build confidence and competing against older kids while holding my own showed me that I was capable of more than I realized. It was a lesson in self-confidence and determination, reinforcing the importance of believing in myself, which was a theme that had become central to my life.

The physical activity was a brilliant outlet for all the tension at home. It gave me a sense of purpose and a way to channel my energy positively. I found a community in my teammates and sports became my sanctuary. It was a place where I could lose myself in the game and leave my worries behind, even if just for a while. Running down the wing with the ball or sprinting down the track, I felt free, unburdened by the weight of the dramas that awaited me at home.

My Penny Panthers and Brisbane Broncos jersey were worn with pride for the school photos and I worked to keep my nose out of trouble, which I succeeded in for the most part. I did take one of the nudist magazines to school for my decoupage project, cutting out and pasting the nude pictures to my schoolbook holder. I had asked Mum first, and she said yes—apparently jokingly—so I did it. I would have loved to be a fly on the wall for that phone call from the principal.

I also got in trouble again later that year when the Courier Mail newspaper showed up to do a story on that legendary bell tower after it caught fire and was extinguished by an off-duty fire fighter. The paper did a full school photo, and someone near me decided to flip off the camera. I swear on pop's grave that it was not me, but the principal wasn't having any of it. The whole school got a lecture and I got the cane. It felt like trouble had a way of finding me even, when I wasn't looking for it. Guilty until proven innocent.

Over the school holidays, I was enrolled in school holiday care since mum and my aunties were working. One of the carers played the movie 'Childs Play 2'. I sat there and watched the whole thing, silently screaming inside. It gave me nightmares for years afterwards. These incidents, though minor in the grand scheme of things, were reminders of the balance I was trying to maintain between fitting in and standing out.

Mum, my sister and I would find happiness in escaping to a day of shopping at the Myer Centre. On more than one occasion, my mum would get so stressed trying to park in city that we would circle around for what felt like hours trying to find a spot, only to give up and leave. Mum's determination to find that elusive perfect parking spot was both frustrating and kind of amusing to me and my sister. We'd have to all chant, "the perfect park is manifesting for us now" until one appeared. Once we got inside, the top floor was epic. It was like stepping into a wonderland for kids. There was a dragon coaster that seemed to loop around endlessly, LEGO displays, arcade games that ate up our spare change, and cinemas where we watched all our favourite movies.

The idea of having a sibling was something I was still getting used to. Her presence meant sharing attention and space. In my eyes she was the favourite, being their daughter. I only found value in my role as the 'big' brother. I remember she had gone to walk past me on the stairs one time and I hip-checked her out of the way. She would have been maybe five and she went flying. She still reminds me of it to this day. I was caught red handed and harshly reminded that I only have one sister and she will be with me for longer than any other relationship in my life, which was a wild thought. Despite the rivalry and occasional squabbles, there was a growing bond between us. After all, she was my little sister and deep down I knew I had a responsibility to look out for her.

I was growing up. Double digits. 10 years old.

Being in the inner-city suburbs had its perks. We would get dressed up and head out to dinner more frequently at places like Kookaburra Café in Milton. The song that sticks in my mind at this time was Bamboleo by 'The Gypsy Kings', which would play every time we went to Montezuma's Mexican in Taringa. I still can't understand a word of the song, but it you can't help but tap your foot when it plays.

My stepfather loved to be the centre of attention. Loud burping or farting when we would go out for dinner, followed by banging the table to cover or amplify the sounds, was a normal occurrence. This used to make me cringe, but nowhere near as much as when he would flirt with the teenage waitresses. They were only a few years older than me. Given that there were always at least two other young women at dinner with us, it probably seemed innocent enough. But I knew it wasn't. My obvious embarrassment of these encounters was clearly noticeable and it irritated him.

To try and rid me of my fear of embarrassment, and as 'personal growth', he would make me perform on stage in front of everyone in the house. I say everyone as the numbers fluctuated between 5-10 people. I truly hated it, but I didn't have much choice. I would be physically pinned there until I did what I was directed to – singing, dancing, telling jokes. If I cried, I was tickled to make me laugh. Not in a fun way, but in a way that still makes me hate being tickled to this day.

On our family nights in, it was much easier to fly under the radar. It would often consist of going to Video Ezy at Coorparoo and renting any true story movie we could find. We would settle in with a fresh batch of plain popping corn—no butter, maybe some salt—and peppermint or jaffa-flavoured carob buds, since we weren't allowed sugar. These nights were meant to be relaxing, but they often highlighted the unique quirks and strict disciplines that defined our family life. On one trip to the video store, I brought a pack of salt and vinegar chips for myself and I was relentlessly ridiculed for my selfish behaviour for wanting something different then plain un-buttered popcorn.

I loved fire. Not in a destructive or mischievous way, but because I was mesmerised by the colours and the way it seemed to dance. I remember I was watching the flame burn inside an old-fashioned oil burner, completely engrossed in its flickering glow, when suddenly I heard a voice call me from the balcony. Startled, I stepped outside just as the lamp exploded, sending glass flying into the ceiling and walls. It was a narrow escape. Seconds before, I had been mere centimetres away from where the shards landed. After the chaos settled, I checked with everyone in the house, but no one had called out to me. There was no one else on the balcony. It left me puzzled and a bit spooked. I'm not saying it was a ghost, but it felt like something was definitely watching out for me that day.

Around this time and for the first time, we had a live-in nanny. Some international students and my elder stepsister moved in for a while. Some of her friends followed. Maybe they were recruited. It was hard to tell. Mum's sister, my actual aunty, also joined us with her two small boys after a messy divorce. I never understood why these women would want to be with my stepfather. He had a way of drawing people in, creating an illusion of charisma and opportunity. To outsiders, he seemed like a successful entrepreneur and projected an image of financial stability and personal growth, which I guessed could have been enticing, especially to those looking for direction or a sense of belonging.

Behind closed doors, the reality was starkly different. He manipulated and exploited those around him, especially the younger women and girls. He played on their vulnerabilities, promising mentorship and guidance while using them for his own gain. For some women, it was about him gaining financial control and using their earnings to fund his extravagant lifestyle. For others, it was about emotional manipulation, creating a sense of dependence that kept them tethered to him.

I struggled to reconcile the image of him as a father figure with the reality of his actions. It was never really hidden. He was grooming the younger ones and sleeping with the mature ones. I even got used to the comings and goings. Some would stay for months, others just weeks. I tried not to get too attached. There were up to 10 people living with us at any one time. So many came and went that I can't even remember all the names anymore.

The one thing I could *never* figure out for a long time was where the money came from to fund his lifestyle. My stepfather 'worked' from home but it wasn't a typical job like my other friends at school's dads. Mum was largely a stay-at-home mother by this point. By this stage they both had nice, newish cars and the house we were staying in was damn near a mansion. I was too young to pick up on the signs, but it became clearer as I got older that our new 'aunties' were being exploited for the so-called greater good of 'The Family.' The women tried to shield the kids from the reality of our situation. Everyone pooled their earnings while my stepfather controlled the money. He insisted on this version of 'trickle-down economics' as the only way to financial freedom.

Robertson

By the time we moved to Robertson, we had a lot of turn over with members in the family. Anyone still living with us were given an ultimatum—put this family above everything and everyone else or leave. Once they finally left, the money dried up as there were fewer income streams. I reckon the ones who stayed got pretty creative with government benefits to make ends meet.

We would have family meetings at any time of day or night, along with random room inspections and changes. I could come home from school to find my room had been swapped with someone else's, and my possessions removed without warning. The level of control and separation was stark. This wasn't just a controlling relationship; it began to feel more like being part of a cult.

To stay, you had to commit 110% to the rules and expectations. Anything less risked being outcast, named, and publicly shamed. There was a constant pressure to conform, to suppress any doubts or desires that contradicted what my stepfather dictated, and to never question anything, as the only acceptable path to success and unity was in complete surrender and subordinance. These tactics created an environment where dissent was not tolerated. Obedience and loyalty were demanded at all costs. Like I said, cult.

It was all extremely rigid and structured. My stepfather sat atop the family apex as the spiritual leader, with his chosen 'brother' a rung below but often privy to the same perks in reward for their loyalty. The women (mothers, aunties, sisters) all took places in the next level of the pyramid as workers, cooks, cleaners and lovers within the family, The children were on the base, essentially acting as walking advertisements for his tried-and-true methods of successful powerful parenting and effective leadership. The women financed the family for years and saw little to nothing for their labour except for violence and intimidation. I don't know and probably never will know the depths or details of it. I was sheltered from so much, but this was simply how I saw it growing up inside the group.

The rules and restrictions crossed over into what we could eat, drink, watch and read. We were not allowed to consume excess sugar, chocolate, soft drinks or flavoured chips. We would take daily shots of aloe vera juice (super healthy, but YUK) and were only allowed carob, which was a sugar-free chocolate. The best you could hope for was a flavoured variety. We were allowed to have homemade un-salted, un-buttered popcorn as a treat. We could drink water or soy milk only. There was never alcohol in the house. For special occasions, we would have a specific brand of sparkling apple juice. There was no watching television during the week, with the exception the family viewing only news and shows considered true stories. On the weekend, music would be the staple viewing on shows like RAGE. Occasionally, my little sister and I would watch the morning cartoons. Reading was much the same. Books needed to be approved and were autobiographical or spiritual in nature.

For those keeping count, this was my fourth school change in six years. The most affluent and multicultural school I had experienced was

Robertson Primary. You would think I'd be used to it by now, but it was still an adjustment. We moved house three times in the next two years while I was there; Metropole Street, Faringdon Street and Devenish Street. The first place was modern by comparison but a massive downsize from our previous digs. The family had all but shrunk back to the core group of five.

Every school change meant resetting my circle of friends. I had long blonde hair and was tall and skinny, just trying to fit in as a pre-teen. I managed to find a good group of mates. I had a quick wit, basketball and athletics skills in my bag and I knew I could use that to connect with a new circle of friends.

My stepfather had set up a basketball hoop set up in our front yard. Despite the ongoing conflict, there was a level of love there. One mate had a detached garage where we could listen to Nirvana and his older brother's grunge CD's. Another mate had an inground pool, so we would split time between all three places, riding our bikes from one to the next. I did try and sleep over at their homes whenever possible, staying up late watching Ace Ventura and Beverley Hills Cop, trading basketball cards and laughing all night. It was almost surreal to see first-hand how their families worked with such normality. They had stable lives and routines that felt like a world away from mine. Those sleepovers were a glimpse into a different kind of life, one that felt calm and predictable. It was comforting and a bit bittersweet, knowing that my life was far from ordinary, but at least I had good mates to share their lives with me. I knew that was the life I wanted for my own family when I grew up.

It was here that I fell hard in love with… basketball. After having my bottom teeth smashed through my bottom lip in a tackle playing footy, I was happy to find a 'non-contact' sport. For the first time, I really threw myself into something and was naturally good at it. It provided me with an escape and a healthy reason to be out of the house. I joined the Sunnybank Tigers as my first ever basketball club.

I would ride to school around 6:30am and play basketball until the bell rang at 8:50. At lunchtime, I was back on the courts, and after school and all weekend too as long as the batteries on my Walkman didn't run flat.

My Smash Hits '93 tape would play all day. For variety, I would stay up late listening to Rick Dees and the Weekly Top 40 on Brisbane's B105FM, pressing the record button on the songs I wanted for my mixtape. Kids these days have no idea of the dedication required to make a mixtape! You had to sit by the radio, ready to pounce when your favourite song came on, and hope the DJ didn't talk too much over the intro. The songs I'd rewind and play again and again were Wreckx-N-Effect 'Rump Shaker' and House of Pain 'Jump Around'. Classic basketball training music.

I was invited to my first ever concert with a group of girl friends (not girlfriends) from school celebrating a birthday. It was at Southbank Piazza, and the band was 'Kulcha'. Honestly, I had never heard of them, but the girl I liked was going and she was a huge fan. There we are in the stadium surrounded by screaming teenage girls for the smooth R'n'B sounds of the band. At the end of the show, they called out 5 lucky ticket numbers to meet the band backstage.... And I was 1 of the 5. While everyone else almost fainted with excitement when their ticket number was called, but I was caught off guard and stuck to decide who to take with me. It was a choice between the girl whose birthday it was and who had invited me, or the girl I was crushing on. I chose the latter. In retrospect, dick move on my part, but at the time I wanted to shoot my shot. If the birthday girl reads this, I'm sorry I didn't swap tickets with you. If it is any consolation, it still bugs me to this day.

Thirty years on, basketball and music are still my outlets.

Those early mornings and late nights were more than just about playing basketball or making mixtapes. They were about carving out a space for myself and finding a bit of freedom in a life that often felt chaotic and controlled. The rhythm of the game and the beat of the music helped me cope with the constant changes and uncertainties. Basketball became my sanctuary. It was a place where I could lose myself and forget about everything else.

But the more I wanted to be a basketball player, the more 'motivation' I was 'supported' with by my stepfather. After we watched Luke Perry in the movie '8 Seconds,' anytime I was hurt he said it was time to 'cowboy up'. If Luke Perry could take a shot to the family jewels from a horse and keep riding, this was now my new minimum expectation. 5am wake-up. 5:15 run. If I wasn't up and ready, a bucket of iced water was poured over me in bed while sleeping (I can't believe people pay for ice baths these days). The soundtrack to these runs was trash talk about how I wasn't "big enough, strong enough, fast enough, or committed enough to succeed". If he could catch up to me, he'd get a kick out of poking me in the arse—not just the cheek, but right in the "date hole," as he called it. The more it pissed me off, the more he did it. It wasn't digital penetration, but wasn't far off.

"Don't let them know your next move."

"Like in a boxing ring, always smile when you are hurting."

I don't want to say it worked, but I ended up going faster than I ever had at East Brisbane and made regionals for the 100m and 200m sprints that year at QE2 Stadium. The thrill of competing at such a level was incredible, and I felt a sense of accomplishment despite the unorthodox methods that got me there. That shock treatment continued for years, and I had to always keep my guard up. Part of me thinks it was his version of motivation, another part leans towards madness, whatever the case it drove me to be better and always competing with myself.

I remember around this time, my little sister had come up to me in tears that a child in her class had kicked her in the privates. Even though I was in grade seven and he was in grade two, I had no issue to right that wrong by punching him in the stomach as retribution. I made sure it didn't bruise, having a pretty good idea by this time where to be hit and not blacken up. Despite our usual sibling dynamics where teasing was fair game, no one had the right to harm or hurt her.

Big brothers often feel a strong sense of protectiveness over their younger sisters, whether they share blood or not. Protecting my sister became a matter of principle; showing her and others that I would always stand up for her, no matter what.

Except for my sister, I became cautious about forming deep attachments and was wary that any bond could be severed abruptly. Even the uncertainty of who would stay or leave our home fostered a sense of emotional self-preservation, prompting me to keep a guarded distance from everyone, even my mother. Friends from school would become distant memories after we moved and I never even attempted to keep in touch. Each departure reinforced the transient nature of connections, leaving behind a sense of impermanence that echoed through my formative years.

Growing up in a household where not everyone shared the same bloodline was a unique experience. It blurred the lines between family and strangers, creating a dynamic that was both confusing and intriguing for a young boy like me. I never quite understood how the relationships formed within our home. The rules seemed to change depending on who was staying with us at the time. We were all expected to put 'the family' above everything else, even if we didn't fully grasp who constituted 'family', but other times it felt like it was every man for himself. I found myself always mentally preparing for the next inevitable change, especially when went from bad to worse.

Sunnybank and Sunnybank Hills

We moved to another few homes in just under two years. Let's see if I can remember. There was Legal Street, Terowi Street and, argh, I'm blanking on the third. I was well versed at uprooting my life. I didn't even unpack all my boxes in those days. The rental on Legal Street connected to the main road of Lister Street in Sunnybank and was up for sale while we were there. My stepfather would rip out the 'For Sale' signs whenever they popped up in the yard in an attempt to stay for as long as possible in the days before internet listings. It was a large, lowset house with a pool, which was a haven during hot summer days. It had a big yard and a tennis court where we put up a hoop to turn it into a basketball court. It had an air of potential.

My school friends at school told me the reason there were so many people from Asia moving to the area was because 'Sunny' was seen as happiness and 'Bank' meant money, loosely meaning 'happy-money' for those overseas investors moving to Australia. If only I had been in a position to purchase it back then. It's now been developed, and the block has been subdivided into three home sites, each worth well over a million bucks. Ironically, we would always rent because the apparent flexibility to not be tied down to one place and his belief that paying interest on a bank loan was like throwing away money. Opportunity kept knocking on the door, but no one ever thought to answer it.

Financially, things must have been tougher than in the family than years gone by. People came and went, but there seemed to be more mouths to feed with no extra income. I stayed behind when the class went on senior camp. I wasn't too worried. I had gone on camp at Graceville and hated being away from my mum. Kids had picked on me for taking my monkey. Being in a cabin with another bunch of new kids I barely knew wasn't my idea of a good time. I figured this would be no different, so I just played basketball and hung out with the handful of other kids who didn't attend, either due to behavioural or financial issues.

The grade 7 graduation ceremony at Robertson in 1995 was a really fun yet sombre occasion. We had to learn a song to sing for the event. Everyone around me was in tears. It must have been their first-time changing schools! We had some great teachers there. Mr. V would play his guitar in class and we would rock out to his version of the Kingston Trio's 'MTA'. We bonded over our love of music.

I remember one of the teachers there was a yeller and would get up close and personal when screaming at your face. He had this one tooth that was pushed back in his lower jaw. You couldn't help but looking at. After growing up with my stepfather, yelling was nothing. In my mind, I imagined this must be what a drill sergeant sounded like. While I had longed for a male teacher to take me under their wing and be a father figure, neither of them fit that billing.

When that house finally sold, we packed up and moved nearby to Sunnybank Hills. Each move brought a mix of emotions. I was excited to explore a new place but the effort of making new friends all over again was always hard. At least this time, all my friends were all in the same situation of leaving primary school and going into high school. Knowing which version of Isaac to be in each situation was still something I was adjusting to. But by now, I had my coping strategies down pat. I would settle in quickly, scope out the best places for playing basketball, and keep my guard up around new faces until I felt safe.

Through all the moves and madness, I learned to find stability within myself and my music. I would put the headphones on, turn up the volume and drift away to the sounds. I had become better at making new friends and mirroring people. I wore my mask better than any superhero's mild-mannered alter ego I knew. I found comfort in the small routines I could control, like shooting hoops or listening to my favourite tunes. I brought my first ever CD single from Cash Converters in Sunnybank Plaza. Jazzy Jeff and the Fresh Prince 'Boom Shake the Room' is still an absolute karaoke classic! These were the constants in my ever-shifting world and the things that grounded me, no matter where we lived.

Now, if you were living around Sunnybank at the time, you would have definitely seen my stepfather running in the mornings in his red, black, and yellow Adidas tracksuit, waving at all the passing cars. He once tried to give a high five to a passing car, which ended in a significant hand injury. He was always loud, proud, and boisterous, making sure everyone knew he was around. His larger-than-life personality was both a source of amusement and embarrassment as a teenager. He thrived on being the centre of attention, often dragging us along for the ride. It was impossible to blend into the background when he was around so I really wanted to keep him away from my new school.

MacGregor High was my pick of high schools. I had done inductions at Sunnybank and Runcorn, but Sunnybank had me in fight or flight mode after witnessing three brawls break out in the one day I was there. At Runcorn, I got lost for about an hour during the visit which was definitely not a good start.

Navigating high school was a whole new ball game. The sheer size of the school was intimidating. This place was HUGE, with almost 2,000 kids. Here, I was a 'veggie'—the nickname for the newbie grade eighters. You had to move from class to class, be on time and it seemed to sprawl out in all directions with buildings that all looked identical to one another. On my first day, I clutched my map and school issued Redbook like a lifeline, trying to make sense of the different blocks and classrooms.

Lunchtime was the real test. The school grounds were buzzing with activity with groups of kids scattered everywhere. I scanned the crowd for a familiar face, but none of my old mates from any of my schools or sporting teams were there. It was a stark contrast to the close-knit community I had left in primary school. I was starting from scratch and trying to find my place in this sea of thousands of unfamiliar faces. Without a group of friends to back me up, I didn't dare step foot on the basketball court against the older kids.

I quickly learned that high school had its own set of rules and hierarchies. The older students ruled the roost, and we newbies had to find our footing without stepping on any toes or risk being flushed. I still remember my experience at Burleigh, and I was not going through that again. There were cliques and social circles to navigate, each with their own unspoken codes. Making friends wasn't just about shared interests anymore, it was about finding your tribe in a much larger, more complex social ecosystem. Survival of the fittest.

In my isolation, I tried to reach out spiritually to my pop. I needed to feel his presence somehow. One afternoon, alone in my room, surrounded by old photos, tears streaming down my face, I silently asked him for a sign that he was alright and asked if he was still around. Suddenly, there was an electricity surge and everything in the house shut off, including the ceiling fan, my lamp and even the TV in the other room. It freaked me out so much that I bolted outside and didn't come back in until Mum got home hours later. Despite the unexpected experience, it gave me an underlying calm that my grandfather was still by my side watching over me. I needed that, because high school had started off feeling really, REALLY lonely.

That finally changed when we went on camp to Tallebudgera in the middle of the year. It was a turning point. There, I finally found an old friend from primary school who introduced me to his circle of friends. They were a mix of basketballers, skaters, and musos (music enthusiasts). After attending so many schools and meeting so many different types of people, I found it easier now than ever before to find common ground with them. Over time, I started to find my groove. I made a few solid friends with kids who shared my love for sport and my knack for a good laugh. We would hang out after school, shooting hoops or just mucking around. Slowly, the massive, intimidating school started to feel a bit more like home. More home than home, anyway.

I threw myself into basketball. I didn't want to be good, I wanted to be great. I wanted to play basketball in the USA. That was my only goal and the courts at MacGregor became my refuge. They were a place where I could escape and just focus on the love I had for the sport. It became my home away from home. I joined the school team and started to bond with my teammates and coach. I was good and they knew it and respected my hard work ethic.

Classes were another adjustment. The workload was heavier, the expectations higher. With all the changes from four different primary schools, all with different curriculums, I realised I had missed large blocks of learning. I felt like I was starting with a disadvantage, especially in maths. In English class, we read a book called 'People Might Hear You' by Robin Klein. I felt there were more than a few nuances between my life and the book and I mentioned something to my English teacher but she was dismissive. I hope the teacher gets a chance to read this book one day and connects the dots. My science teacher berated me in front of the class a few times for not understanding theory, being more of a practical hands-on guy myself, until I threw my textbook across the room at his head and walked out. My music teacher was pretty and never wore a bra, so my mates and I would ask for help on the keyboard. Constantly. We never got much better, but we always enjoyed the help.

I had some wonderful teachers during my time at MacGregor High from 1996 to 2000, several who I still think about to this day who helped guide me and look out for me. They got me through some tough times. They probably never knew the extent. I will never forget them for that and want to take a moment to say thank you. They had supported me and influenced me so much I went to do grade 10 work experience as a physical education teacher at a school in Greenslopes.

Outside of school, I would have to navigate the fights that would breakout in the laneway running adjacent to the Highway, between the High School and the bus way. At least in those days, it was somewhat structured. You would know where and who would be fighting. There was an unspoken rules of engagement with this stuff. It was always one on one. Once you were knocked to the ground, you were done. If these rules were broken, bystanders would step in to break it up. No weapons. We kept them for bigger group fights.

To make things work, I had to learn to juggle my studies with my growing commitment to basketball. It was a balancing act, but I was driven by a desire to prove myself, both on the court and in the classroom. Within 12 months, I had moved up from the C grade team to A grade and got selected for the Southern District Spartans Rep team. The highlight was playing in the annual Classics tournament held in Knox, Melbourne over the Easter break in 1996. My coach was really considerate, since I was still a strict vegetarian and to be as inclusive as possible, the team would eat at Fasta Pasta for every dinner. Back in those days the food court options consisted of a felafel kebab, ordering the roast vegetables from the carvery or a whopper with cheese but no meat. (You can imagine the looks you would get... *'you don't want the meat!?*) Twice a week, after grabbing a quick feed, I'd catch the 598 bus from Garden City to Carina Bus depot, then race across to the baseball fields to Southern Districts Basketball Stadium for training which ran from 4-6pm.

On the weekend, my family would come out to watch and sometimes film the games, which was fun. The only time my stepfather came, he called out every missed shot and remind me how many points I would have had if I was better. Nothing like hearing, "1 miss, 2 misses, 3 misses – bahahaha!" yelled from the bleachers and sounding like a smug 'Count' off Sesame Street.

Another of my coaches at the time was the head coach of John Paul College. He has asked the question 'if' I was ever offered a basketball scholarship, would I be willing to transfer to JPC? It felt like he was sussing me out without formally asking the question. I went home buzzing with excitement to tell the news to my mum who scoffed, "no child of mine will go to a catholic school". End of discussion.

That Christmas, Michael Jordan's 'Space Jam' hit the screens and set the stage for a '3 on 3' basketball tournament in King George Square in Brisbane City. We chalked up a few wins that day, but fell short of making it to the finals. The movie's soundtrack blared on repeat for a solid eight hours over the two days. I even met a girl there, who was a gun player in the girls' comp. It turned out to be a milestone for me. I got my first ever phone number. The next day, I called her up, keen to get to know her better. In our chat, we discovered something mind-blowing. We lived in the same suburb, on the same street! In a sprawling city like Brisbane, spanning 15,000 square kilometres, we were mere hundreds of metres apart. It was destiny. A romance quickly ignited, and she was my first kiss.

Growing into a teenager, I was being exposed to stuff inside the house I wasn't ready for. When my stepfather found out I had a girlfriend, he offered to show me how to 'do it'. He said I could watch him do it with my mum or aunties to learn a thing or two. Keep in mind, I was only 13. When I declined the offer, he provided me with access to his video tape collection instead. I am not talking about softcore stuff either. It was X rated 25+ VHS tapes. He would swap them with… yep, you guessed it, his 'brother'.

It really affected my understanding of what was normal or healthy in intimate relationships. It was commonplace for me to see the man of the house have multiple women share his bedroom. Nudity in the home was as normal as making breakfast. Videos titled 'freaks of nature' were on rotation and openly accessible to me. It had seemed 'cool' and grown up at the time, but looking back, I was way too young to be exposed to that level of adult content.

The arguments between him, my mum and my aunties got more and more vocal and violent, escalating to physical fights. It was often over little things, like them being on the phone too long or the potatoes being too hard at dinner. Plates would get thrown. Entire meals would be simply binned. Mum was a great cook and always made our dinners with so much love. Seeing this thrown back in her face was heartbreaking. I still miss her roast dinners. She would spend hours preparing kidney bean burgers, cauliflower cheese, roast veggies and a fresh salad with homemade dressing. It takes a special kind of cook to make a strict vegetarian diet taste good... EVERY. DAMN. DAY.

I started to withdraw from my mum around this time because private conversations I would have with her would be relayed word for word to my stepfather. The 'black hand' would be wielded accordingly. To paint the picture, he would sit behind his desk, Mum at the door blocking the exit and I was stuck in the corner with nowhere to go. It was a similar story for anyone else under our roof. Private conversations, secret thoughts or feelings and commitment called into question could be used to get into my stepfathers favour by taking someone else out of it. Calls were listened in to on his private line, notepads could be shaded over to see what was written on the previous sheet of paper and you had to have eyes in the back of your head at all times to make sure nobody was hiding around the corner spying on you. I learnt to tune into the volume of the house to find out what the mood was as soon as I walked in the door. Sometimes it was easier just to turn around and walk out again.

MacGregor

New chapter, same school, but here's the plot twist you never saw coming; I actually did the full five years of high school at MacGregor High. It was the longest stretch of stability I had ever had. Before that, I'd never been in a house, school, or neighbourhood for more than two years. The house churn didn't stop, though. We moved four times over the next four years, but at least it was all within the same area. Literally a 1km radius! Carnaby Street, Luton Street, Darlington Street and Leadenhall Street. School had become my refuge. I had a solid friendship circle, found my niche, and it was just me looking out for me. My little sister was still in primary school, doing her own thing.

I would walk from home, down through Henderson Park, jumping the Mimosa Creek, (only on dry days, because when it was raining that creek was more like a rapid) up onto Blackwattle Street and MacGregor High was right there. I would go directly to the basketball courts.

Basketball meant the world to me. I would literally play every day of the year, no matter the weather—rain, wind, or sunshine. Our courts were outdoors, but that never stopped me. After I'd walk to school, I would spend over three hours each day practicing. Weekends, school holidays and even Christmas Day you would find me there. In Year 10, we clinched the Brisbane Metro championship with a thrilling 47-45 victory over Tullawong

High. We were trailing by five points with just a minute left on the clock, but we mounted an incredible comeback. I top scored with 20 points and was honoured with the school's MVP award. It was one of the greatest moments of my life up to that point. Victory was made even sweeter because their crowd had chanted, "faggot, faggot!" every time I touched the ball. During those crucial free throws in the final minute, I responded by blowing them a kiss. I never backed down on the court.

I injured my ankle playing in the Classics in 1997. Coming down the court on a fast break with one defender in the key, I planted my foot to hit him with the spin move and my whole body spun, except my foot. The medics had to cut off my Fila Grant Hill Sneakers, which was heartbreaking because they were my lucky pair and I had to go to hospital after having the green whistle. I have always been superstitious when it comes to basketball and I am very strict about my pregame routine, including my sneakers.

In 1998, I missed out again due to injury. This time, I injured my left elbow after coming down hard on a dunk attempt. It was frustrating because I'd been training hard all year, hoping to redeem myself after the previous setback. I kept pushing forward, determined to get back on the court and make my mark in the next season. Honestly, in retrospect, I reckon I hit my peak around age 16.

The members of 'the family' were always in flux but my first ever aunty, who was more like a godmother to me, grew closer to me over the years. While others who had the opportunity to leave did so, she stayed by my side, always watching out for and wanting to protect me. Our long drives out to her family farm in south-west Queensland in her 1970s silver Sigma, with its leaking bright green coolant fluid, was time alone with her that I cherished. The journey out there felt endless, but her company and the escape from my everyday life were priceless. At her family farm, her mum would whip up fresh butterfly cakes and lemon butter, while I would search through the fields for old farming antiques and crystals. Being included in this intimate circle of her life made me feel incredibly special. She did more for me than she will ever realize. We had never discussed what she went though to keep me safe, but I will always love her for it. I truly believe I owe her my life.

Psychologists talk about this phase in a boy's life when he is transitioning to manhood as a time when you're really trying to find your own identity. I was pushing boundaries, exploring new things and butting heads with Mum over decisions 'the family' was making that directly affected me. But in the middle of all that awkwardness, there are moments I remember that really strengthened our bond. For my 15th birthday, all I wanted was a gold chain. Mum surprised me with a matching one to hers, but instead of giving it to me on my birthday, she hid the 14ct. necklace inside a nibbled-out Easter egg. I found it while unwrapping Easter gifts, and it's still one of the best surprises I've ever had. These moments kind of grounded me and showed me that despite the challenges, there was a deep love and connection that still tied us together.

Meanwhile, my stepfather was becoming more unhinged as he got older. He became more controlling and more threatening as I grew from a headstrong boy into a stubborn and strong young man. He would often tell me, "Your death wouldn't ruin my day". I remember it was just after my 15th birthday and we had some type of bust up. He threw me into the kitchen brick wall and, for the first time ever, I clenched up, ready to fight back. He saw the anger in my eyes and told me, "Take your best shot. I will put you in the fucking ground". To be clear, this wasn't 'on' the ground, it was 'in' the ground. From then on, I started sleeping with a pair of scissors between my mattress and wooden bed slats, if he came for me, I wasn't going down without a fight.

We knew he could snap and kill any of us at any time. Especially if we tried to leave. Mum, in particular. When a fight grew loud between them, I would push myself in there to intervene so he would leave her alone and turn his attention onto me. I could always take the beatings better than the others. Physical pain wasn't an issue. I could block that out. It was the emotional pain I struggled with. One night, he sent my mum to the hospital after she lashed out at him. He threw her into the ensuite mirror. She put her hands up to protect her face and sustained some deep cuts to her wrist.

After this, mum tried to leave with us a couple of times. We would get dressed like we were going to school, pack up what we could into our school bags and go searching for a rental we could afford. Women's shelters wouldn't take us in because of my age and gender, so we had no choice but to return. We had no relatives to stay with. We had moved so many times, we had never retained any friendship group outside of the family members. We knew if he found us, the consequences would have been death. Staying became the lesser of two evils.

It was at this age that I first had the idea that if shopping centres had a space where all the services were together—Centrelink, financial aid, legal advice, rental assistance options—maybe mums with kids trying to escape domestic violence could get all their help in the one spot, without having to run around town and worry about being seen or traced. Back then, the cooking and grocery shopping was seen as 'woman's business'. I thought that having these services all in one place at the shopping centre just made sense. There's security, cameras, plenty of people around with safety in numbers and it was not unusual for a woman and her children to be seen there.

This idea stuck with me, and about 20 years later, it became an Australian first concept and the proudest moment of my professional life called Magnolia Place; a partnership with StandbyU Foundation where a regular retail shop within a major shopping centre was converted with the sole purpose of helping connect people with services and reconnect family and support networks. Essentially, I was trying to get protective services to intervene before situations escalate and instead emergency services are called to respond to the scene of a crime. It's based on the idea and my lived experience that it takes a village to raise a child, so why not create a village to save lives?

Around this time, a friend of my older stepsister's had moved in down the street. She was a recently divorced schoolteacher and had a young daughter who was about seven years old. She was only a 'part-time' part of 'the family'. Another 'aunty' had moved back in with her two kids. In a way, it was nice to have more people around again and larger groups often defused the tension better. Or more accurately, the abuse was simply spread around between more people.

As a teenager, I was allowed 1 x 15-minute phone call per weeknight. It was often listened in to on the second landline. Even though there was no TV allowed Monday to Friday, I found WCW wrestling on late night TV and loved sneaking down to watch Goldberg matches with the volume down low after everyone had gone to bed. I loved re-enacting some moves and stunts at school and once even power bombed my little sister onto the bed with such force she bounced through the flyscreen on the window (which she never lets me forget) but it was all in good fun and we both had a laugh. We got dial up internet and thought it was the greatest invention ever. It sounded like a CT scan and would get disconnected if someone picked up the land line to make a call. I could record whole songs from the computer. Sure, it would take all night to download a song but because I had it with no ads, there was no rush to hit record like on the tape deck. LimeWire and Napster were the OG's and earliest, most infamous file-sharing platforms, particularly known for their role in revolutionizing the way digital music was shared and distributed online today. While I enjoyed mum's CD collection of The Doors, Santana and Fleetwood Mac, if not for downloading songs I would have had ZERO chances of buying, let alone listening, to Rage Against the Machine, Limp Bizkit or Tupac.

That computer's life was short-lived however after an axe went smashing though the screen in a fit of rage from... guess who...

I met my first love when I was in grade 10. She was a beautiful hippy who radiated happiness and had the most amazing smile and caring nature. Her mum and stepfather were really welcoming and had a great chill vibe about them. They had a swimming pool in her townhouse complex and that was the first place we kissed. We would love going to the movies together and simply hanging out. She brought a calmness to my life and for the first time, my attention at school wasn't solely fixated on basketball. We would hang out at each other's house and would make out in my bedroom until the day my stepfather burst in the door and physically pulled us apart. We were each other's first, but within a year she had moved away, changed schools and we lost touch. As fate would have it, we randomly reconnected years later when I was on a trip to the Gold Coast and she is one of only a handful of people from this time in my life I am still in contact with. The song that reminds me of her is Dru Hill's 'How Deep is Your Love' from the CD single she gifted me for Christmas in 1998.

My stepfather's creepy or suggestive words and behaviours would often scare off friends and girlfriends that would come over to our family home. I guess I had become somewhat numb or accustomed to the oddities of my life, even though it was in stark contrast to theirs.

I have these nostalgic flashbacks of the high school crew, like the times we'd gather our tables and chairs into a square we called 'the pit'. We had this playful pretend gang called the 'MacGregor Mafia', partly as a joke in response to a local gang called the '18 Angels' who had tagged our school. It was at this phase in my life when I rocked cornrows and drew 'tattoos' on my arms in permanent marker. Yep, true story. It was a bold fashion choice back then, influenced by the music and culture we were all into at the time. Thank you, Allen Iverson, the toughest player pound for pound who I tried to shape my game after. Remember that song 'Pretty Fly' by Offspring? Yep. That could have been written based on me.

I had a few really good friends through this period, but my best mate was Stoney. We had been largely inseparable since grade eight. Despite us coming from completely opposite backgrounds, we found an unbreakable connection with our similarities. We used to joke that together we were the 'Rock and Stone' connection. His dad was a pastor, and his mum cooked the most incredible Indian food you could imagine. I practically lived at their place, crashing there as often as I could. His mum even jokingly called me her third (white) son.

We thought we were so cool, cruising around Stones Corner and the City or walking all the way from Garden City to Sunnybank. We'd hang out, dressed like we were a part of a boy band from that era, go shopping, listen to music that we couldn't in our respective homes, try to talk to girls and support each other's big dreams and crazy ideas. With him by my side, I felt invincible, like I could tackle anything. We'd walk to school together almost every day, and no matter what chaos was happening at home, he had this knack for always putting a smile on my face. Whenever I hear Will Smith's 'Men in Black' theme, it takes me right back to those days. We once even performed that dance from the music video on stage for a talent show and that same year were both chosen in Year 10, by our principal, to mentor the new year eight kids on a bonding camp. It was a huge honour as just 10 of us in total, 5 girls and 5 guys, were picked for our leadership qualities, or in my case, knowing exactly how far I could push the boundaries without getting in trouble.

In high school, I did push the boundaries too far a *few* times with pranks I thought were hilarious. I was suspended once for forging a report card after I managed to get my hands on the stickers the teachers used and wrote my own sexually suggestive messages. I ended up doing community service for that one. The playground at MacGregor Primary was proudly painted by yours truly.

I was also suspended for my first side hustle. I realised boys my age wanted to see porn and since we couldn't watch VHS tapes at school, I would go to the second-hand bookstore and purchase nudie magazines for .50 cents each. I'd buy up a ton, keep them in my school bag and then sell them for $5 each. I could only get my hands on the softcore Picture or People mags, but they were more than enough for the other kids at school and was turning a profit of $4.50 each time, until I got caught.

I suspended myself from drinking after New Years Eve. Never again. Not like that. Five of my friends and I had a house party at a girl's place after watching the fireworks at Mount Cootha from my mate's vintage Toyota Supra. We had bottles of Jim, Jack and Bundy and only about 4 litres of Coke between the group. Drinks started off fine but as the mixers ran out, we just started taking shots from the bottle. We were all wrecked. I went to the toilet at some point, threw up on myself and remembered thinking a cold shower would sober me up. I did that and promptly passed out. When I came to, I was freezing and couldn't find my clothes or a towel, so I grabbed the floor mat and wiped myself down. There was a hairdryer on the bench and the cord from that became my makeshift belt. I was sick the entire next day and think it was January 2nd before I emerged from that room.

I was kicked out of the local shopping centre on multiple occasions. When fights would flare up, we would tip the shopping trollies on their side, jump on the middle part of them and the metal handlebar would pop right out. I would keep the metal bar in my mate's car or my school bag in case things got out of hand. I also learned life skills for how to break into a car using nothing but some commercial packing tape or a cars antenna. I got busted once getting caught in a compromising position in a changeroom with my girlfriend. While another time I was accused of taking a fast-food meal off the counter that wasn't mine. I was marched up to the centre management office and told they had me on camera. They didn't believe me when I told them I had been vegetarian for the past decade and when I asked for the footage and was told I couldn't see it, I called BS. They handed me a ban notice for 7 days.

Funnily enough, 18 years on from this, I was employed in a senior role looking after that same shopping centre. I always found it hilarious they let me back in. Amazing what a suit, tie and change of name will do.

Mum thinks we bumped into my real father once at Garden City while I was in my high school uniform, but she didn't tell me until later that night. We were walking down the mall together when they locked eyes. He looked at her, then at me, and apparently darted away. She didn't give chase and I can only imagine if it was him, he must have been doing the timeline math in his mind after glancing at me and recognising Mum. I didn't notice it, so I guess that sliding door moment closed with me none the wiser.

Sunnybank Plaza became my sanctuary my refuge, especially the basketball card shop run by a guy named Wayne. He was an absolute legend. The last time I saw him a few years back, he'd moved on to working in an electrical store. I used to think he'd be a perfect match for Mum. I thought having a stepfather with similar interests who was kind and polite would be just what we needed, but looking back, I realize I was pretty naive. His shop wasn't just a place to buy cards; it was where I could unwind, chat about hoops, and escape whatever was happening at home. He had this way of making everyone feel welcome, whether you were there to buy cards or just shoot the breeze. It was a bit of a haven during those teenage years, where I felt valued and welcomed.

There are 3 things in life I have always dreamt of: seeing my name in lights, playing basketball in the US, and becoming the dad I always wanted.

My little sister was part of a dance and performance centre in Mansfield and through there was introduced to the world of acting and modelling. I started tagging along with her, and soon enough, they asked if I had any experience in the industry. They were short on young boys for their roster and invited me to join. Got some head shots and within a few weeks, I landed my first paying gig as an extra on the TV show 'Medivac'. That opened doors to recurring roles on 'The Wayne Manifesto' and 'Cybergirl'. Acting felt natural to me; after all, I'd been playing roles all my life.

As time went on, more opportunities came my way. I did extra work on films including 'The Great Raid', 'Fools Gold', 'Inspector Gadget 2', 'Blurred', 'Through My Eyes', 'The Punishment', and I even had a few lines in 'Peter Pan' that unfortunately ended up on the cutting room floor. This opened doors to appear in several radio and TV commercials also which was great pay. Acting became a way for me to explore different lives, experiences, and expressions far beyond what I had imagined growing up. I'd take my roles very seriously and try to ensure that casting would invite me back with dreams of landing bigger roles.

My first 'real' job was at Franklin's Supermarket when it opened in Sunny Park. I was almost 15 and started off as a checkout chick, decked out in the classic white business shirt, clip-on tie, and cap. It was a fantastic place to work, and over time, I worked my way up to supervisor and eventually found myself in the cash office in the years that followed. One time, I had a close call with a potential hold-up. Unbeknownst to me, I struck up a conversation with the person who turned out to be armed. Thankfully, I didn't realise it at the time. In the end, he ended up robbing another place nearby. I'd like to think it was because I showed him some empathy, but it was probably because my cash float was only $300.

I was known for never calling in sick to a shift. Even with a busted jaw that had swelled up so much you couldn't see my ear, I was back at work the next night. Despite numerous injuries sustained, including multiple concussions, I always pushed through.

One memorable, though blurry incident involved taking a softball hit a few millimetres from the temple, knocking me out cold. It was crazy to wake up and see colours you had always known inverted. The poor student teacher who was taking our PE class at the time was kneeling over me while I regained consciousness saying, "Isaac, Isaac, do you remember your name?" I was like, "ahhh... Isaac?" She looked more shaken than me! I dusted myself off and insisted I could go to basketball training that night but was told I needed hospital instead.

Another time, during a training drill, I crossed over a teammate and ended up taking a headbutt to the jaw, resulting in a hairline fracture.

There was another frightening moment when I blacked out from heat stroke and dehydration. I've broken both thumbs and pinky fingers at least once, chipped my elbow, busted ribs, some sweet scars cut open above my right eye and even chipped several teeth along the way. Despite the pain and setbacks, I was determined to keep playing and working. That was my stepfather's philosophy: it's not about how many times you get knocked down, but how many times you get back up.

Working as much as possible was crucial to me. I had a once in a lifetime opportunity coming up, in the annual state basketball tournament where there was a selection of players from across Queensland to be picked to travel to the USA representing Ipswich Basketball. It felt like my years or training and dedication has been leading to this and I had learned from previous team trials take nothing for granted and leave it all out on the court. That roster spot was mine. For a month, we'd be competing against high school teams over there, aiming to secure a scholarship to an American university all kicking off on New Years Day in January 2001. To make it happen, I needed to save $3,500 for the trip and another $1,500 for the car of my dreams. $5 grand in total.

After tax, 30 percent of everything I earned went straight into paying board. The rest was carefully divided into savings envelopes hidden behind my bedroom door. Each envelope had its purpose. Food, going out, clothes, car savings, registration, insurance, travel, savings etc. I had my sights set on my first car, a 1983 Mazda 323 with all-electric windows and power steering. Always have goals and targets to work towards, no matter how big or small it'll provide focus and motivation.

I finished high school in the year 2000. Our graduation ceremony was held at Brisbane City Hall, which held a special place in my heart since I attended childcare there back in the early '80s. 'Hells

Purple Flying Dishwashing Monkeys' was the name of the band we put together for our end-of-year twelve breakup. I took the stage as the lead singer, belting out Limp Bizkit's cover of 'Faith' in front of the entire grade. It was a wild moment that I'll never forget, though looking back at the video tape, I wish I could.

The high school experience all in all was a really positive one, what started off lonely evolved into this whole new world. I found my tribe, I was fortunate enough to mesh with different groups of friends, sporting, creative from the art, film and while I have never mastered an instrument always appreciated the musicians. I would trade my lunch box fillers with kids from different nationalities and ethnic backgrounds to try new things. Mum made my lunch so good I don't think I ever had or wanted tuckshop. By the end of my time in High School I knew my way around like the back of my hand, the make out spots under the art block, smokers in the D-block toilets (not that I ever partook), shortcuts from the oval to skip school and not get caught. Early on I had no desire to go to school dances or parties. Mum forced me to go, in my eyes they ate into basketball time, however once I actually went and experienced it, I found I really enjoyed it. It added to the high school experience. A few of the boys and I would stay up all night at the movie marathon events held at the cinemas over the holidays, four movies, one night and no sleep. I made some genuine long-time friends here and while we aren't in touch as much these days it's comforting to know they are always just a call away.

After graduation, the same group of six of us who had shared that notorious New Year's Eve in '99 ended up going to schoolies together a few days, it was a bit of a buzzkill so I came back early to pick up some extra shifts for spending money. My focus was squarely on the next big adventure: the USA! The tour took us through an incredible itinerary: San Francisco, Oceana, Lodi, Lake Tahoe, Sacramento, Reno, past Area 51 to Nevada, Las Vegas, and Los Angeles. Over 27 days, we played 16 basketball games and stayed with host families in most towns. There was a memorable hiccup in Lake Tahoe where an administrative error landed us in a hotel instead of with a host family. I vividly recall sitting in the spa on the roof with snowflakes falling on my face. Coming from Brisbane, that was mind-blowing. First time seeing snow.

We landed in LAX, blurry eyed yet pumped with energy and anticipation, the first photo I took of this eye-opening culture shock was a homeless man, pushing a trolley full of bags with one hand and holding a gun in the other. Welcome to LA. The Australian dollar was around .49 cents to the US $1, so we had to be savvy with our spending money. We found joy in exploring free activities, the newspaper stands in Vegas were a laugh and simply soaking up the accents, atmosphere and cheap food —it felt like a home away from home. The trip was packed with so many unforgettable experiences. We were thrown parties, visited Universal Studios, Disney, University of Cal State and Stamford, and caught NBA & College games. It truly was the time of my life and a dream come true that I never thought I would achieve. The level of skill, speed, and toughness in the games over there was eye-opening, something I couldn't fully grasp until I experienced it firsthand. So many talented players over there are working to break out of poverty and bring generational wealth to their families, they had more to play for than we did, and it showed. Playing in Lodi was an amazing experience, they joked they were famous for wine and Credence Clearwater Revival getting stuck there and writing a song about it. The game we played there was packed to the rafters and was my best game of the tour before getting a chest infection. One of the guys on our tour got asked to stay on scholarship; he was such a pure scorer and went on to play in the NBL, which was so cool to watch from the crowd in later years. In the moment though we were all celebrities or felt like it anyway. Being interviewed, appearing in local newspapers, swapping jerseys and keepsakes.

One of host families I stayed with introduced me to Linkin Park and I was instantly hooked. Their CD played on repeat throughout the entire trip. Two years later, I had the incredible opportunity to meet the band backstage at Livid in Brisbane in 2003 and even got photos with Chester and the whole band. Those memories from the US trip remain some of the most cherished moments of my life, filled with friendships, adventure, and experiences that I never thought a kid like me could experience.

While I was in Reno, I found out via email that the family I have known for the last 12 years was breaking up, and had to be out of the house before the end of the month when the lease expired. That snapped me back to reality pretty damn fast and put life in context. Upon arriving home, I found everyone had already moved out. It was just me, my room and my stuff to box up and move. It was surreal. The house was so quiet. My stepfather had blamed it on my little sister after a massive family fight. I suspected if it ever happened, it would be when I wasn't there. Sure enough, I was right.

So here I was, returned from the trip of a lifetime, the pinnacle of my hard work and dedication. I was still hoping for an acceptance letter into university in Brisbane, when suddenly I find out my family has split, I am essentially homeless, all within a few weeks. To top it off, Centrelink sent me a bill for repaying youth allowance from the time between high school finishing to university commencing.

From the highest of highs to the lowest of lows. Life comes at you fast.

Main Beach

My mum and sister moved in together at Tarragindi for a short while before relocating down to Newcastle to start over. I get it. She had been beaten down and controlled within the strict confines of the family for the last 12 years and needed to find herself and this meant getting out of Brissy. Newcastle was a near 15-hour overnight bus ride away for me.

My stepfather moved in with another aunty nearby, however it was short-lived after an alleged incident with her young daughter. He ended up back in East Brisbane, living with some young international students who didn't speak much English and paid all the rent. That was the last time I ever saw him.

My aunties scattered and went into hiding, with nothing to show for the years of work except for the clothes in the bag and their old beat-up cars. Everyone fled when they saw the writing on the wall. No goodbyes. No notes. Just gone. I liken it to a pool table break with everyone once clustered together just scattered. I know it was done for self-preservation, but to not have a family or place to live at the age of 17 was a difficult time in my life.

Fortunately, I had a lifeline and moved in with my High School girlfriend, her mum and two younger sisters who were living nearby to where I was working. I admired how big their family get togethers were and how they were so uneventful by comparison to my experience. I even did birthing classes with her cousin who was a single mum, so she didn't have to do it alone like my mum circa 17 years earlier.

My girlfriend and I were on again, off again and the pressure of suddenly living together coupled with the fact we both had too much lived trauma to help each other was a recipe for disaster. When she found photos of me with a girl in Lake Tahoe during the US trip reunion, things ended pretty quickly. That time. We would be on again and off again for a couple of years trying to recapture that spark we had at the start but never could trust each other. I realise with the benefit of hindsight, I was constantly looking for love and approval to fill a void in my self-confidence.

During the peak of our fights, I had turned to self-harm to deal with the stress. I was not cutting, but I would knock myself out to end arguments. Not healthy and I'm not proud of my actions here, but I need to share for context. I never hit her or anyone else. I would take the anger and frustration out on myself. I now have major concerns for CTE as I get older. Between these and sporting head knocks, I can recount around 10 occasions where I have lost consciousness. I'm not going to lie. In the moment the empty darkness felt good. The splitting headache afterwards was an easier pain to handle than the emotional ones I couldn't compartmentalise.

I was in a tight spot financially having spent all my savings on my first car, the stunning Mazda. She was my pride and joy and I taught myself to drive by spending my nights navigating the carpark of QE2 Stadium. I had my learners, but I couldn't afford the driving lessons, so of a night I would sneak across to the stadiums mostly empty carpark and practise parking, reversing, and driving around. The car was my ticket to freedom, but that freedom only stretched as far as I could afford to go. I needed my own space, my own place to regroup and ended up looking at a caravan park in Springwood as about the only place I could afford on my own at the time. It wasn't ideal, but I thought it might be a temporary solution. Even the onsite manager handling the rental suggested I look for other options, which says a lot about the state of the place.

The original plan was to attend university to study design, in particular product design, however the required OP score went from a 14 in 2000, to a 4 in 2001 due to popularity. I submitted my portfolio and a letter from my high school art teacher supporting my enrolment hoping to get a special allowance, but I was not accepted. I looked at TAFE options but studying without a safety net, full time job or stable home just seemed impossible.

Earning or learning had always been my goal. Earning it would have to be. The Franklins I worked at closed their doors and despite being re-employed at the Carindale shop, there were only twelve hours a week work available for me. I needed to find something more. My high school basketball coach reached out to me to see if I would be interested in a coaching role. She was coaching the seniors and wanted me to coach the grade 10 boys' team. I had to get a blue card and would be paid for the role (though I am still not sure if that was via her personally or the school) which involved taking one training session and coaching one game a week. I loved being back on the court. In some manner, it was so hard to be on the sidelines with every fibre of my body wanting to play. The boys came together amazingly and ended up with a very solid team that did really well. I still see a few of them around and share some memories. They were good kids, all grown up in their 30's now. My coach had thrown me a lifeline and gave me a cause, direction, something to look forward to. Thanks Fi.

After the hours at Carindale dried up, I landed a new job working as a barista for a new coffee shop franchise. They were opening in Sunnybank which was way closer to the place I was staying; but to do training I needed to work from their operational shop in Main Beach on the Gold Coast. My first four weeks were unpaid training, the first fortnight shifts were the opens starting at 5am, and the second fortnight were closes getting out around midnight. I couldn't afford to pay for petrol driving the 60 minutes each way to and from the Gold Coast plus my living arrangements were up in the air anyway, so I regularly just slept in my car at Main Beach. The downside was cars are very cold to sleep in, which I didn't realise prior. Some nights I would shiver so hard it would make me throw up. The upside was though, I had ocean views! When I had enough money from tips, I would stay at a youth hostel a few blocks away for $10 a night. Food was readily available from the cake cabinet after closing but before the vegetarian panini sandwiches were thrown out. Found out the bakery nearby donated all their unsold stock each day so managed to charm some bread and basics there too. Some of the local café workers found out and let me crash on their couch which was kind of them. They didn't really know me or owe me anything. This arrangement lasted a few months and despite sounding shitty, it was a really free time of life. I was back by the ocean watching the sunrise over water and setting in the hinterland. I still keep a backup bag in my car if I ever have to sleep rough again, but this time with a warm, wool lined jacket.

I clearly remember where I was as the events on September 11 unfolded. I was watching TV and I thought it was a movie, right up until the second plane hit. I remember sitting there in stunned silence watching throughout the night as the situation kept escalating what felt like every 30 minutes. I think everyone remembers where they were when they found out feeling completely helpless in such a terrible situation. I know I did. The USA was so close to my heart and one of the only places that felt like home at the time from my trip only months earlier.

Eventually, I came back to Brisbane when the café opened. I spread my time between their shops at Sunnybank, Taigum and Victoria Point. I was getting paid $7.75 pre-tax per hour, and I was keen to work as many hours as I could. I was finally old enough to sign a lease and rented a room in a share house in Acacia Ridge. While it was the single, two-story home all five different rooms were leased individually between $80 to $120 per week. We had shared bathrooms, laundry and kitchens, and everyone had to park out front because the garage had been turned into a makeshift meth lab by one of the guys living on the lower level which I wasn't thrilled about.

Times were tight, I would steal toilet paper from public bathrooms, to afford new clothes, I would take two items into the change rooms and carefully swap the price tags, I would still pay, but at a lower price. I would borrow CDs from the library and buy old second-hand VHS tapes for $1 than hire a $6 new release as my weekly treat. I knew I needed to make a change when at the end of one hard week all I had left to eat in the cupboard was a tin of four bean mix.

This was the make-or-break point. I couldn't keep living like this.

Which leads me to the Bridge. It is honestly difficult to replay this night in my mind. It was a dark time. I have never felt so alone, unwanted, and unloved in my life. No one knew the real me, myself included. Sunset had come and gone. I remember watching the horizon turn a bright orange hue and then fade to darkness. It felt like my energy and outlook on life, which once were bright, had faded fast and would soon turn to black.

Mum was in another state with my sister. The aunties had moved away and started a new life. My girlfriend and I had split again, so I was on the outer with her family. Everyone I had known and loved in my whole life had left or, in my mind, abandoned me. I was a distant memory in their rear-view mirror and no one was looking back.

I was broke, unemployed, and with no stable place to call home.

I was at rock bottom and there was no roadmap or preparation to navigate myself out of this mess. This wasn't the plan. I had dreams for playing professional basketball that had washed out. My backup was studying design but I didn't make the grades. I couldn't even get my life together enough to afford my own place. It seemed everything I had worked and hoped for was evaporating right before my eyes.

I had walked this overpass hundreds of times; from my safe space at Sunnybank's card shop, to shopping days with Stonie and my first two jobs were either side of the overpass. It had been a fixture in my life for the past 7 years since we moved to the area in '94. I climbed up and sat on the edge, watching and wondering. If I jump now, would anyone notice? Would anyone miss me? How long would it take before someone, anyone, realise I was gone? My self-loathing and pity were at an all-time high.

Weighing up my options, I kept trying to gage the height and outcome. If I jump is the fall high enough to kill me? Maybe I should try and time it for one of the big trucks that race up and down Mains Road, but that hardly seems fair to transfer the guilt of my suicide into their hands. Maybe I aim for that blue guardrail separating East and West traffic? I imagined getting impaled but not dying. That would suck.

Running through my mind were all the times my stepfather had reminded me that I wasn't strong enough, tall enough or committed enough to make it. The bumps and bruises had healed but the words still rang loud in my head. I couldn't turn the volume down, so I started saying them out loud. Very loud. It flipped a switch inside. It was a lightbulb moment.

HE didn't think I was strong enough, tall enough or committed enough. But that was HIS thoughts, not mine. I never wanted to be like him, so why would I listen to and believe all the crap he dumped on me? In that moment, I realised I was going to live for myself and to hell with anyone who wasn't on Team Isaac. There was only one person I could trust or depend on, and it had been that way for years. I just hadn't seen it at the time.

Just like tomorrow's sunrise I vowed to shine so bright one day and that journey started as close to the end as I had ever come. I would never stand in another man's shadow. It was me against the world. I had to back myself. I drew my line in the sand that night and I have never looked back.

Mum never could understand why I felt so connected to the Sevendust song 'Live Again'. The passion in Lajon's voice ignited a rage inside me that won't let me quit. It speaks to me on a cellular level. Every time. Even to this day. *"How many times have you looked at yourself and felt mistreated? How does it feel to know that this life of yours is real? All of your life you've been led to believe your nothing, so look at yourself and start to live again!"*

For my birthday, my mum bought me a bus ticket to visit her in Newcastle. It was literally the longest bus ride of my life, travelling through the night from Roma Street in Brisbane. When I finally arrived, it was heartening to see that Mum and my sister had made a life for themselves there. Newcastle had a very arty vibe and Mum had settled in with a new guy. They all seemed happy enough, starting fresh with just the three of them.

We had banoffee pie and coffee while catching up, talking about their new lives and what Newcastle was like. This visit felt different. What really got to me was the realisation that I couldn't be the big brother protector anymore. My sister was having a tough time settling in, and I was 600kms away. The dynamics had shifted, and I wasn't really part of this new chapter in their lives. But as nice as it was to see them, I realised Newcastle wasn't for me. My life was firmly rooted in Queensland.

Runcorn

Nothing is going to change unless you make the change. That mantra stuck with me through thick and thin. At the time, the coffee shop had given me the training and skills I needed. They didn't want me to leave and even threatened me if I did. But I had an ace up my sleeve. I had a damning note from the franchise owner who once told me to never hire any "Asian, fat or ugly people," despite the fact the main store was in Sunnybank, an incredibly diverse area.

When this handwritten direction from the owner came to light, they let me go with all my entitlements. I took this opportunity and my new skill set to throw myself into multiple jobs. I worked relentlessly: from 5am to 9am at a health café in Central Station, Brisbane, then from 3pm to 10pm at another coffee shop in Sunnybank, Monday through Friday. On weekends, I juggled shifts in the cash office of the newly opened Supermarket in Algester after friends from my first supermarket job had reached out to see if I was free. Sign me up.

Seven days a week, over 10 hours a day. It was gruelling, but it lifted me out of the spot I was in.

The hustle was intense, but necessary. I needed to break free from the constraints of my previous job, living arrangements and mental health and prove to myself that I could do it. The early mornings in Central

Station were a blur of coffee orders and busy corporate commuters, I'd take the train from Runcorn station to Central in the darkness, but I learned to master the art of the perfect latte and started to enjoy the routine. The evenings at coffee shop were a different pace—busier, more social splitting time between front of house and the kitchen duties. Whatever needed doing I was there for, and I found myself connecting with regulars who appreciated a friendly face after a long day. Weekends at the supermarket were a whirlwind of numbers and transactions, but it felt good to be part of something new and growing. Working in the cash office again reminded how highly others thought of me, still a teenager but given the responsibility of hand counting over a hundred grand a day. I had to balance that float to the decimal point before I could clock off for.

Hospo work is fast-paced, and time flies. I've always loved it. I moved around a lot within the industry looking for the best work and social environment, the one I spent the most time in was up at Garden City where I had grown up though high school. The café had its fair share of drama, like the time it came to light that our German manager, got fired after taking the night's takings to the casino for days on end. The banking would either be late (if he won) or never deposited (if he lost). Tips and everything, just gone. It was a reminder that integrity is everything, you can change jobs but your reputation sticks. You must protect that above all else, there are no short cuts to success.

It was also here that I learned to never make a chef angry. The back-of-house consequences were not for the faint-hearted. Ever seen a man make love to someone's steak? I have, and it's not pretty.

Speaking of making love, it was at this café that I met my wife. She was a regular coffee customer, and I was the barista. But our connection wouldn't take place for a couple of years yet. Meanwhile, there was a girl I really liked at the time who worked alongside me, but she had a partner, so our relationship was a bit of a secret, and I dedicated The Killers' 'Mr. Brightside' to it. I'd get butterflies just being around her until she relocated to Canberra taking up an opportunity too good to pass up there.

Around this time, I moved in with one of my best mates who had grown up playing basketball with since the mid-90s. He was on that first big basketball trip to Knox in '96 with me. I still remember the day he got his licence; he came around to pick me up from MacGregor on his maiden voyage, and we cruised around like we owned the world. We scored this two-story townhouse together, and it was an awesome setup though minimal furniture (not by design) it felt like a legendary bachelor pad in my eyes. Living with him was a blast. We had a great dynamic, and comradery we even got back into basketball together at Southwest Metro. Our townhouse became the go-to spot for our mates. Whether it was impromptu basketball games in the front driveway or all-night movie marathons, there was never a dull moment. As life would have it, he ended up meeting a girl at one of our house parties, moving in with, and eventually marrying her, breaking up our epic setup. I couldn't blame him, but it was the end of an era.

We used to head out to either Hotel LA on Caxton Street where they'd have five free drinks for hospo workers when you produced a payslip on a Monday night; while Thursday was student night at Mary Street Nightclub in Brisbane with $2 shots and you could almost *guarantee* that Rage Against the Machine's 'Killing in the Name' was the closing song played by the live band in the downstairs bar. There was a core 3 or 4 of us, 20 bucks in hand for the bus, drinks and either kebab or pizza slice afterwards. I would always be the last one standing screaming the lyrics back at the band in the mosh pit. It was my way of letting it all out. The raw power and rebellion in that song deeply resonated and while we didn't know what therapy was, this was our form of it, shouting out our frustrations, feeling the music reverberate through our bodies, and getting lost in the moment. Those nights were about more than just having a good time; they were about finding a release.

Truthfully though, after that NYE lesson I never got drunk to a point I couldn't jump into action if needed, I always kept my wits about me to be the protector of the group. I never slept around having one-night stands either I didn't want to be like my biological father and not be there for my kid. I just loved the music, my mates and being present in the moment to enjoy it all.

Holiday and highlights at the time were when one of my best friends and her family would let us use their holiday home up the Sunshine Coast. We would need to board a train, then take a bus and a short walk to grab some groceries before settling in for the week. A group of six of us would stay there every year during the holidays, it was awesome. One memorable night, we were playing truth or dare, and I was dared to do a nudie run. Tipsy Isaac was more than happy to oblige, so off I went, running down the street, around the surf club, and back. Just when I thought I had successfully completed the dare, I felt something sharp in my foot. I had stood on a bottle and managed to cut the inside arch of my foot. So, there I was, holding my bloodied foot in one hand and my privates in the other, hopping back to the holiday house. I think we got some paper towels and gladwrap to seal the cut and MacGyvered it shut. Good times.

As nice as the Sunny Coast was our day trips down to the Gold Coast were always my favourite, it was like coming home for me, the goldy is where I had my first full family.

We would start the day early to beat the traffic, grabbing hot cakes and hashbrowns from the Maccas drive through on the way south. We'd roll the windows down, crank the music up, and let the wind blow through our hair. No matter the weather or time of year, we'd always find our way to the beach. There was something grounding about feeling the sand between your toes and hearing the ocean rolling in. It seemed to wash away all the problems and stresses of life. There was a particular spot near Burleigh where we loved to go, free parking right on the water and the waves were perfect, vibe was always chilled and welcoming. After a few hours in the water, we'd lounge on the sand, soaking up the sun and sharing stories. Lunch was usually fish and chips from a beachside takeaway, eaten straight out of the paper while watching the world go by. There's nothing quite like the taste of fresh, salty chips, dripping in tomato sauce with the ocean in the background and the occasional rainbow lorikeet screeching overhead. Sometimes, we'd wander up to Currumbin Creek, exploring the rockpools, rainforests and waterfalls that felt like a world away from the bustling coast despite being a twenty-minute trip.

Those day trips were more than just a break from routine; they were a reminder of the simple pleasures in life. The freedom of the open road, the beauty of nature, and the joy of good company made every trip special. We'd stay until the sun started to set. The drive back was always a bit quieter, everyone a little tired but content, replaying the day in our minds. These trips taught me the importance of taking time to recharge and appreciate the natural beauty around us. Whether it's a spontaneous trip to the beach or a planned hike in the mountains, those moments of escape and reflection are what keep me grounded and ready to face whatever comes next.

I found a great little a one-bedroom apartment in Nathan behind the Griffith University campus. This was my first ever home where it was just me. A couple of mates helped me move in and source some furniture. I found a brown, almost velvet material twin seater lounge on the street from council curb side cleanups. I picked up a dining table setting from the trading post to fit out the house. It wasn't glamorous but it was mine.

Mum and her Newcastle partner split up, so she moved back to Brisbane with my sister and got a place in Runcorn. By this stage, I had been out of home for three years. I didn't feel like I was a big brother to my little sister anymore and I felt more like a friend than a son to Mum. It was nice to have them back. I felt more whole than I had in recent years, but it wasn't the same.

I was still my sister's protector when I could be or when she would let me. She found a boyfriend who was a local drug dealer and user. He had beat up on her and when I saw the bruises, I went to his house to confront him. He hid in his bedroom and moved his bed behind the door so I couldn't kick it in. My sister pushed me out of their house to protect him. I couldn't stand by and watch this continue to happen, but I couldn't make her change either, so I had to walk away. I never gave up on her, I just needed to give her space.

Family bonds are some of the strongest ties we experience in life. The connection between a mother and daughter, or a brother and sister, is built on love, trust, and a shared history. But what happens when those bonds are tested? When someone we love is trapped in a damaging situation, and despite our best efforts, they refuse to see the truth? Sometimes, the hardest and most necessary step is to cut ties, even if it's temporary. I cut my ties with my sister, just like my grandmother had done with my mother. People are quick to tell you that blood is thicker than water, but blood when tainted becomes septic and even fatal if not treated.

This lesson taught me something I still hold onto. I cannot control anyone's rate of change any more than I can control the wind. It can't be sped up or slowed down. It changes at its own pace, regardless of what anyone says or does.

After working multiple jobs for several years, I decided it was time to take a leap of faith and back myself into a new pathway in sales with the ability for earning a commission. I applied for a role, working with a company on behalf of pay-tv subscription service. It was a high-risk, high-reward scenario. If I failed, I couldn't afford my rental and I'd likely be back to living out of my car, but if I succeeded, there was a base salary, commission, and good hours. We earned twenty bucks for a renewal, a hundred for a new connection, and there were additional bonuses for achieving ten new connections in a week.

One of the benefits was being able to watch four TVs at once and getting free membership, which was a pretty sweet deal – though I never took up the offer, I figured if it was there, I would watch it and I needed to use my time wiser than that. The pressure to hit targets led some people to do shady things—like reading the obituaries and signing up recently deceased individuals, paying their deposits, and forging contract signatures to chase those weekly bonuses. Another copied someone's credit card details to buy concert tickets for him and his friends, but I kept my nose clean and stayed true to my principles. There are no short cuts to success.

While working in Browns Plains, I bought Alter Bridge's album "One Day Remains" I still have it, and it's one of the best CDs I've ever heard from start to finish. I can't pick a single favourite song because it was the soundtrack to my life in these years.

Our work parties were great fun and one night the crew decided to celebrate with a dinner at a place called the Tibetan Kitchen in New Farm. We had a lovely waitress who only had one eye. When it was time to pay, the cashier asked where we were sitting, and my mate spun around to point to our table. In the process, he accidentally poked the poor waitress in her one good eye. She dropped like a sack of potatoes, and we rushed to her aid. Thankfully, she was okay, and we bought her a drink to make up for it. We all ended up laughing until we cried.

My hard work paid off, and I was moved into a team manager role, then onto an area manager role. Over the span of two years, I saved enough money to buy a newer car my 1994 Nissan Pulsar which had been my dream car since taking my learner's test in one. To celebrate this new chapter in my life I planned a trip back to the USA. It felt like a significant milestone, being able to revisit many of the locations I stayed at back in 2001.

Returning to the USA was surreal. I had grown and changed so much since my first trip. Visiting places like San Francisco, Las Vegas, and Los Angeles brought back a flood of memories, but with a new perspective. I remembered the excitement and uncertainty of that first trip, the dreams of playing basketball, and the hopes of landing a scholarship. This time, I wasn't chasing a dream but celebrating how far I had come and figuring out who I was at this time of my life.

That trip was my first solo adventure and my first-time backpacking. Over six weeks, I journeyed from the west coast to the east, exploring Los Angeles, Denver, New Orleans, Miami, Tampa, Orlando, Atlanta, and back to LA. The experiences were incredible. I got to see Game 1 of the Miami vs. Detroit NBA Eastern Conference Finals in 2005, saw Carlos Santana and Los Lonely Boys play in Tampa, and even snagged a photo on Puff Daddy's Rolls Royce in South Beach for Memorial Day Weekend. In Hollywood, I met Paris Hilton after the House of Wax premiere and encountered the most amazing collection of characters from all over the world —Germany, Israel, the USA, and Australia!

In San Francisco, I was able to reconnect with some of the host families who had looked after us during the basketball tour. Seeing familiar faces and sharing stories about our lives in the years since was incredibly warming. We had left lasting impressions on each other, and it felt so good to reconnect. I met a fellow traveller in Hollywood, who was originally from Melbourne, and we ended up having a cliché holiday fling that saw us reconnecting in multiple cities and even back home that Christmas. It was spontaneous and exciting, adding another layer of adventure to the trip.

New Orleans was surreal, a melting pot of blues music, hurricane cocktails, deep south food and voodoo magic. Many people were talking about big storm season, but when Hurricane Katrina hit only weeks later, seeing the city underwater was simply heartbreaking. The vibrant streets I had walked through, now submerged, was a stark reminder how quickly things can change. It was a place full of life and culture, and the devastation that followed was a sobering reality check. Miami was like something straight out of the movies, I don't think I slept there was so much to do, and South Beach was such a stunning city. I found a cheap car for sale and drove up to Orlando using a colouring map of Florida found in a Subway restaurant as my roadmap. Then, it was north to Atlanta before leaving the car and keys outside of the airport carpark and jumping on connecting flights to LAX and home to Australia.

The trip also allowed me some much-needed relaxation and reflection. An accidental undertaking figuring out who I was on my own. I spent time soaking up the sights, taking in the vibrant culture, and having some spending money for shopping. There was something incredibly fulfilling about revisiting those places as an adult, with more confidence and a clearer sense of direction. It wasn't just about reliving the past but about acknowledging the journey and appreciating how each step, each struggle, and each triumph had led me to this point.

Coming home, I felt revitalised. In addition to the beach, music and basketball, travel was my newest happy place. I had new energy, and I needed an outlet for my creativity, so I decided to study graphic arts and printing at TAFE. It was the first time I'd gone back to studying since leaving high school five years earlier. To support myself, I picked up my old café job, which was now under new management. The flexible hours allowed me to balance work and study effectively.

Meanwhile, one of the other bartenders and I came up with a side hustle. We started doing paid, private bartending gigs, wearing only aprons for house parties. It was a 'cheeky' way to make some extra cash, and we always had a good laugh doing it. Each party was different, and we met some colourful characters along the way. I always had a side hustle. I always loved finding a way to make things interesting and getting a little extra cash on the side always helped.

Studying was a refreshing change, the courses in graphic arts and printing sparked my creativity and gave me new skills. It was exciting to be learning again, and I felt a renewed sense of purpose and fulfillment. The balance of studying and working made life busy but rewarding. Each day was a new adventure, whether it was creating designs, connecting with people while serving coffee, or planning our next bartending gig.

I came close to moving to Melbourne to be with my LA woman (yes, it's a sneaky Doors reference—one of the top five bands of all time) after she came to Australia for Christmas 2005. We'd been keeping our relationship alive despite the long distance for the past six months, and when she landed on Aussie shores, it felt like no time had passed. I headed down to Melbourne to spend some time with her and her family, camping along the Murray River. It was a beautiful setting, and being out in nature was a perfect backdrop for our romance. The days were filled with laughter, boat rides and waterskiing, while nights were spent around the campfire, cooking and reminiscing and dreaming about the future. Despite how perfect it felt, the timing was just off. She had to return to the USA to finish her studies, and as much as I wanted to make it work, I couldn't ask her give up on her dreams for us. It was one of those moments where everything felt right, but life's timing and circumstances pulled us in different directions.

Back at the bar, I hired this incredibly cool Canadian chick to work at the café alongside me, and from the moment we started chatting, it was clear we clicked. She was (and still is) one of the most genuine, no-nonsense people I've ever known. She'd give you the shirt off her back without a second thought. We were both in similar situations, carving out our own paths without a family safety net nearby. It was like finding a kindred spirit who understood what it meant to build your own life from scratch. We had each other's backs through thick and thin, and that bond only grew stronger over time.

Fast forward 20 years, and she is not just a friend but an integral part of my life. She's the godmother to my three children and was a bridesmaid at my wedding. She remains one of my closest and most trusted friends. Despite the passage of time and changes in life, our friendship has stood the test of time. In the early days, my mum was concerned about our friendship. She had this idea that guys and girls couldn't just be friends and warned me that it wouldn't end well. But we proved her wrong. Our friendship was built on trust, respect, and genuine affection, and it has only strengthened over the years.

Looking back, it's clear that she was a rare find. She is a friend who has been with me through so many stages of my life. Our bond has been a constant source of support and joy, a reminder that true friendship doesn't adhere to any rules or boundaries. It's about connection, understanding, and the shared experiences that make it all worthwhile.

Mum's feedback made me take notice of an unfolding pattern within my relationships. Every time things would start to get serious with a girl, it felt like my mum would intervene in some way. It wasn't always overt, but her influence would manifest in various forms—sometimes as an explosive life event, other times as an unexpected crisis that seemed to conveniently arise just as things were heating up. I'd be getting close to someone, and suddenly, my mum would have some sort of dramatic episode or issue that demanded my attention. It was as if, subconsciously or not, she had a knack for creating turmoil right when things were about to get serious in my personal life.

At first, I brushed it off as mere coincidence. But the more it happened, the more I began to question whether it was just bad timing or something more deliberate. There were at least three girlfriends who shared their concern with me and it felt like there was always something pulling me back just as I was trying to move forward in a relationship. I couldn't help but wonder if it was all just a way to keep me tied to her or to keep me from moving on. It was a frustrating and confusing experience, especially when I was trying to build a life with someone else.

This pattern made me realise how deeply entwined my relationship with my mum was with every aspect of my life, including my romantic relationships. It wasn't just about dealing with her; it was about trying to balance my own needs and desires with the emotional chaos she seemed to bring into my life. I had to learn to set boundaries and figure out how to manage these situations without letting them derail my relationships. It wasn't easy, but it was a necessary step towards understanding the impact of these patterns and finding a way to move forward in a healthier way.

Woodridge (Logan Central)

This place was wild. I lived a few blocks down from the train station and the Logan Diggers club on Ewing Road. The IGA would often get robbed, and there were stabbings in the adjacent park. Walking home from the train station was almost a guaranteed ticket to a scrap. You had to always keep your wits about you. With my surroundings as they were, we didn't go out often, so I really dedicated myself to cooking and really loved making up some of mum's old recipes and my own favourites.

Meanwhile, my mum had moved in with a new guy. He seemed nice, a patched motorcycle-riding, pot-smoking hippie who was completely anti-establishment. He had a place down in Loganholme and a block of land in Cornubia. Together, they bought this little fixer-upper in Woodridge. They asked me to move in so they had renters they knew and could renovate without too much pushback or red tape about access. It was cheaper than my place at Nathan and had two bedrooms so served as a place for my friends to move in with and get on their feet.

One of those friends was a Brazilian dude whom I met and formed an instant bond with while he was housemates with members of a punk band on the Goldy called New School Hero, they had a great song on their EP called, "Gotta Go". He was a 6'6 and a gentle giant, we'd go out together to catch live music at the Diggers or a cheap feed. One night we came home to find his room completely full of dead bees—hundreds of them. We filled several takeaway containers full. We had no idea where they came from or how they got in there. I think we settled on voodoo as the only possible explanation. We would stay up watching the Dave Chappelle Show and Family Guy, laughing our heads off ignoring the chaos outside. My ex from high school stayed for a while during the final phase of our off again, on again relationship – everyone would joke we were like Ross and Rachel from Friends, and even my little sister moved in after bouncing between her mum and dad's place for years, I was overjoyed to finally have her with me and being able to watch over her.

I kept a baseball bat over the front door for when people tried to break into the unit or cars, or if one of my sister's exes came by to stir up trouble. It was a necessity, I felt, to keep my home and loved ones safe. My car had been broken into several times, but the most that was stolen were some empty CD cases. Back in those days, we had CD head units that we would take in and out of our cars to prevent the stereo from being stolen and a wheel lock to keep the steering wheel from being able to turn while installed. It was more of an inconvenience than an insurance claim, but it was still annoying.

Living in Woodridge was an experience. It was a rough neighbourhood, but it had a certain raw 'charm'. The local characters, the constant buzz of activity, and the sense of being on the edge—it all made for an unforgettable time. There was never a dull moment, and while it was challenging, it also felt like we were all in it together, navigating the chaos and finding our own way. But having my friends and fam around made it feel like a real community. We supported each other through thick and thin, shared our highs and lows, and made the best of what we had. Despite the rough exterior of Woodridge, inside our little haven, we found moments of peace, laughter, and genuine connection.

A friend's cat had a litter of kittens I adopted one who needed extra care, the runt of the litter I named Simba. This beautiful black part-ragdoll had a deformed front leg, which made it difficult for him to walk in a straight line or flick his kitty litter properly. No buyers would take him due to the leg; it wasn't an injury; it was just him. He looked like a furry gangster, crip walking everywhere he went. Simba quickly became the mascot of the house, a constant source of entertainment and companionship in a neighbourhood that was often anything but.

Taking care of Simba was my first adulting responsibility, looking after something entirely on my own. It was a significant step for me, having something rely on me for their wellbeing. Despite his physical challenges, Simba was full of life and had a playful spirit that was infectious. He would hobble around the house, he couldn't really run, jump or climb but managed to get into all sorts of mischief, his unconditional love made me forget about those tougher times.

Simba was more than just a pet; he was a reminder of the importance of perseverance and the ability to find joy in the little things. Taking care of him taught me patience and responsibility. I had to make sure he was fed, clean, and up to date on his vet check-ups and shots, which gave me a sense of purpose during a time when life to that point had seemed so chaotic.

As the month went by, we developed a routine. He'd sleep on the end of my bed and wake me up in the morning, tapping my face with his little paw, and I'd feed him before heading off to the gym and work while in the evenings, he'd curl up on my lap after dinner while we watched TV or studied. Everyone loved him, it was impossible not to!

The fixer-upper was a constant project. True to my unconventional life to date, the unit's renovations and expectations were no different, when the bathroom got re-tiled, we'd have to drive 10 minutes and use the gym facilities at Sunnybank Hills to have a warm shower which went on for a couple of weeks. But we adjusted and made do. I would watch my mum's partner DIY and learned a lot from him including a spirit level is not in fact called a leveliser, and we turned the backyard into a bit of a covered junglescape playground for Simba.

I can't talk to the relationship between him and Mum in much detail, but from what I saw, they were happy. He was different to my stepfather growing up; much more inclusive, less domineering and for the first time it looked like an actual partnership. I never lived with them but would visit weekly and they eventually got married—Mum's first official time, as far as I know—and I was involved in the ceremony. He essentially became my second stepfather. Mum took his name and that was the third change of name for her. They both seemed pretty happy and it was great to see mum happy again.

He taught me a lot, particularly about using power tools. One Christmas, he gave my sister and I our own set of power tools and lawnmower. I thought it was the best present that year. My sister was nowhere near as impressed. Not every teenage girl wants a mower after all. He was a hands-on guy with a knack for fixing things and an entrepreneurial spirit. His love for conspiracy theories was endless; he could talk for hours about the latest one he'd come across. But what I remember most were our movie nights. He loved watching the Tropfest short films and would have Wilfred on repeat, laughing out loud the entire time. One of his favourite lines from the film was, "You can never have too much cheese on nachos," and he'd say it every time we made it, having a good laugh.

His influence extended beyond practical skills and quirky humour. He introduced me to the world of independent films and Australian cinema. Our movie nights became a regular bonding activity, and through them, I discovered a shared appreciation for idea sharing and creativity. No one had ever really listened to my ideas before. Neither he or mum had completely cut off from their hippie roots (which I loved), their Loganholme house was decorated with nude images on most walls and they were really open about their pot growing, even bragging about it to his daughter's partner one night, who was a cop.

The Cornubia land had multiple cars, boats, and workshops within a few large sheds. The block of land was on a few acres, it had a big dam (we'd call it a billabong) and eucalyptus trees so dense you could barely see through. When they tied the knot, it was on this block of land. It was the first time in twenty years my nan, my mum, her sisters, and their kids were all together again. It was almost like our first ever family reunion and would ultimately be the last.

It was hard to establish where the truth in their relationship lay. I know there are three sides to every story, but my mum would often vent to me about their arguments and issues. Within days, things were 'back to normal' and whatever concerns I had were dismissed. "I am over it, so why aren't you?" was the attitude. With the added exposure to drugs, my mum's mental health seemed to decline. She confided in me that he had guns and if she ever went missing, he had killed her. I couldn't tell if this was real or an exaggeration, but the fear in her voice told me there was something serious underpinning this belief. Mum's anxiety was palpable, and it wasn't something I could brush off easily.

Runcorn part Deux (like Hot Shots!)

While working at the cafe, with my best mate as my wing woman, I met a girl who was studying teaching at Uni. She would come in all the time with a guy, and I never made a move assuming they were together. One day, he told me they were not a couple (wink wink), and when she asked me to borrow a pen with her coffee order one day, I took the opportunity to ensure the napkin had my mobile number written on it and the coffee had a love heart design on top. Just like Rob Thomas and Carlos Santana I was so 'Smooth'.

I had a few rules for finding a quality match when dating. The first is what's known as the door test; another piece of life advise pinched from a film called 'A Bronx Tale'. Open the passenger car door for the lady to hop in, walk around the back of the car and peer through the rear window. If she leans over to unlock your car door, she is a keeper. The next rule was to see if she would acknowledge the checkout operator or cashier after the first date. After all, I was a cashier only a few years earlier and a simple smile, chat and thanks goes a long way. And the final rule was that I couldn't date someone who smoked, did hard drugs, drank to excess or swore more than me. I am a sucker for a natural pretty face. A gorgeous smile and kind eyes are the things that you'll be looking at for years to come. I appreciate these rules won't work for everyone, but they worked for me to ensure I found a partner on a common wavelength and someone that could build a foundation based on shared values before taking that next step.

Our first date was to be a casual one. Saint Patrick's Day was right around the corner, and I mentioned there was a staff party she should come along to. To my surprise she said yes, so I had to quickly try and organise a party. When that fell through, I had to say plans had changed, and we instead spent the night at a café in West End. As the night went on, we moved from playing chess to walking around, exploring its nightlife and vibrant street art. We shared stories and talked all through the night, her openness and honesty were refreshing. She was genuine, kind, and had an adventurous spirit that matched my own.

It turned into one of the most memorable nights of my life. The casual atmosphere of the café, the strategic intensity of chess, some random kid who joined in and showed my date how to wipe the floor with me in the game and the deep conversations we had about everything under the sun created a bond that was hard to ignore. I had never stayed up all night just getting lost in conversation, her smile and eyes captured me, and her passion for teaching and making a difference in the world was inspiring. Despite the initial fear of getting too close, I found myself drawn to her more and more. She challenged me, was smart, knew what she wanted and ready to embrace the possibility of a future filled with love and happiness. With her, I didn't have to pretend or put on a facade. I could be myself, flaws and all, and she accepted me for who I was.

We sparked immediately, and for the first time about a month into the relationship, I wanted to run away. I didn't feel like I deserved this happiness, this love, or this feeling of safety. It was kinda foreign to me. But she had a way of making me feel at ease, breaking down the walls

I had built around my heart. Our connection was effortless and being with her felt like finding a missing piece of myself. This felt real. Like *really* real.

Over the next few months, our relationship blossomed. We spent countless hours together, whether it was studying at the library, hiking in the mountains, or simply watching movies on the couch. She quickly became an integral part of my life, and I loved every moment we shared. There were still moments of doubt, where I questioned what the heck she saw in me or I was ready to settle down. Afterall, I had never seen how to have a stable, loving and peaceful relationship. But her unwavering support and belief in me helped to slowly dissolve those fears. She taught me that it was okay to be vulnerable, to lean on someone, and to trust in the goodness of what we had.

Wanting to share this exciting news with my mum, I invited her over to meet the parents. It was supposed to be a pleasant lunch, a chance for both families to get to know each other and for Mum to see how happy I was. However, it turned into an absolute trainwreck. She arrived without her partner in a cloud of tension, and I could tell she was already on edge. We sat down for lunch, and the initial small talk was strained. Her parents were warm and welcoming, doing their best to include Mum in the conversation. But she seemed distant, her responses clipped and guarded.

Halfway through the meal, as my girlfriends mum was sharing a light-hearted story about their travel, Mum suddenly burst into tears. The room fell silent, mum stood up abruptly, something about feeling overwhelmed and feeling they were rubbing their 'happy family and easy life in her face'. Before anyone could really react, she stormed out of the house. I ran after her, calling out, but she got in her car and drove off, leaving a cloud of confusion and leaving me to try and explain the outburst in her wake. When I returned to the table, her parents were understanding, but the atmosphere was irrevocably changed. My girlfriend squeezed my hand, trying to offer comfort, but I could see the concern in her eyes while I tried to hold it together.

Later, I called Mum to check if she was okay, but she didn't answer. It took a few days before she finally picked up my call. She was evasive, not wanting to talk about what had happened, only saying that she felt out of place and overwhelmed. I tried to reassure her, telling her that they were lovely people who had a back-story also, and that they were excited to meet her again when she felt ready, but she remained distant.

This was a stark reminder of the complexities in my relationship with Mum. She had always struggled with letting go and seeing me happy with someone else perhaps triggered her fears of losing me. Despite the tension, I knew I had to set boundaries. My emerging relationship was important, and I couldn't let mum's insecurities derail it.

My partner came to stay at my Woodridge abode a few times, I always loved cooking and showing off my domesticated skills and Simba was a lady killer, but I could tell she was uneasy. It wasn't because of our new relationship but the late-night noises throughout that neighbourhood. It became clear that we needed a safer, more stable environment for the three of us. Soon, it was suggested that we move in together to her unit in Runcorn down on Glenefer Street. So, Simba and I packed up and joined her there, leaving behind the chaos of Woodridge and passing the torch of unit minder to my little sister.

Living together was a fresh start. We discovered our mutual love of sushi train, often indulging in it as a treat. Our evenings were filled with laughter as we watched episodes of South Park and cheered on our favourite wrestlers in WWF, we would watch pay-per-views at a friend's place, where my mate would make the most epic homemade pizzas while my partner tutored their eldest daughter in maths. These gatherings became a cherished monthly tradition, blending fun with the warmth of friendship and feeling like a 'real' couple and watching how they juggled three kids. Our circle of friends rapidly changed my high school friends who were still single, and partying seemed to drift away while we started getting closer with other couples from my basketball squads who were on a similar relationship trajectory.

She became my guide in navigating more affluent social settings tutoring me on how to act and behave appropriately, the nuances of etiquette, how to use a knife and fork properly, though I still prefer to swap hands. Advised me to avoid controversial topics like religion, politics, and conspiracies at the dinner table and to steer clear of asking other couples about their plans for marriage or children. These lessons were invaluable as I began to move in different social circles, ensuring I didn't unintentionally offend or alienate anyone. As crazy as it sounds, despite the strict rules within my family growing up these things just never formed part of our lessons or structure.

As our relationship flourished in Runcorn, we created a comfortable and loving home together, balancing our interests and supporting each other's goals. Simba adapted well to the new environment, becoming a beloved part of our little family. We were about six months into the relationship, spending the day at the beach when she confessed that she had met someone at work and felt a connection with him. He must have been a good-looking rooster; she was flattered by his interest while being confused about her feelings and uncertain about what to do about it. It took me by surprise, but I knew I had to handle it maturely.

If you love something, you should set it free, right? I read that in a book or saw it in a movie (more likely), anyway, I suggested she go on a date with this guy, hoping that afterward, she would realize it was us

Runcorn part Deux (like Hot Shots!)

who were meant to be together. It was a gamble, but I believed it was better to face this potential issue now rather than years down the track. I'd rather know after six months than six years. I didn't want her to stay with me out of obligation or fear of hurting my feelings.

Taken aback by my approach, I believe in that moment she realised I cared for her happiness above my own and realised that was a rare find in this world. The experience while bittersweet at the time brought us closer together and reinforced our commitment to each other. From that point on, we navigated our relationship with renewed clarity, transparency and understanding. We continued to grow as a couple, facing challenges together and supporting each other's ambitions. Our bond became stronger, rooted in trust and the knowledge that we had chosen each other freely, without any lingering doubts. Balls on the line, but it played out the way I had hoped.

With the new relationship, new home, I landed a new job. A real job. Working for an iconic Brisbane brewery. I had to give up my TAFE study and occasional audition and acting gigs, but I missed earning real money and the freedom it provided so I finished part way through my Certificate III in graphic design and printing.

The week I started, my mum went missing.

Their marriage had been volatile recently and my mum had moved in with my sister at the unit in Woodridge. I helped mum to move some her stuff across and since I had left most of my furniture couch, fridge, and washer at the unit. My sister had a fully furnished place and I was still paying off the interest free loan on the white goods, so Mum offered to purchase them both for $500. We would speak daily, but on a winter Saturday night few weeks later, Mum's phone was going straight to voicemail. No one had seen or heard from her all day.

The first place I checked was the unit and found her asleep in bed, or so I though, I got up close and realised it was just pillows stuffed in the sheets in the dimly lit room. She had either slept there the night before or it was made to look that way. I called her husband's mobile phone. No answer. Called their home. No answer. I called their neighbours, but they hadn't seen either of them. And that's when I remember mum telling me - *if she ever went missing, he had killed her*. It was replaying over and over in my mind. I called the hospitals to see if she had been admitted under any of her names or aliases. There were at least five she'd go by, but still nothing.

I went into Mt. Gravatt Police Station to file a missing person but couldn't because she was an adult and it had been less than 24 hours. I frantically drove down to their house to find no one there and all the lights off. It was late by now, past midnight, and I had only one more place I could think of; the block of land at Cornubia where they got married. There was a large dam or billabong on the block, and he often worked late there.

It was almost 1am when we got to the land, flashlights in hand, looking for any activity or signs they were there, but it was all dark. No signs of movement. No signs of life in the workshop or any of the regular places. The realisation hit me that I needed to search the dam. I rolled up my jeans and very quickly was knee deep in this muddy, boggy water, feeling for my mums' corpse. My girlfriend was holding my hand, so I didn't become fully submerged. She was riding shotgun by my side every minute. The neighbours came out with torches to see what the commotion was and suggested we leave and come back in the daytime. We were wet, cold and scared but they were right. There was nothing we could do but wait for daylight and answers. I didn't sleep that night and just paced the unit thinking of anything I might have missed or any place I hadn't checked.

About 10am the next day, I received a call. My mum and her husband had gone away for the night, in secret, to rekindle their relationship. They didn't want anyone's judgement, so they did not tell us, leave a note or keep their phone on. "Don't overact!" was the statement that floored me. "My happiness is important too, you know!" WHAT THE ACTUAL!?

That night, through the turmoil and uncertainty, my girlfriend had stayed by my side. She held my hand firmly, offering comfort and reassurance as I grappled with the emotional rollercoaster. Despite the chaotic mix of feelings and the difficult situation, her unwavering support had shone brightly. She stayed positive, focused on finding my mum and keeping my spirits up. It was a testament to her character that she had the ability to remain calm under pressure and supportive during one of the most stressful times in my life. Her presence was a balm to my worried mind, and her dedication to our relationship was evident in every action and word.

As we navigated through the feelings of that night, I couldn't help but reflect on how much she had become an integral part of my life. The way she handled the situation with such grace and empathy made me realize that she was not just a partner, but someone who truly understood and cared for me on a profound level. In those moments of vulnerability and support, I knew with absolute certainty that she was the one for me. Her strength and compassion reinforced my belief that we were meant to be together. She had proven herself to be not only a loving partner but also a rock during times of crisis. Our bond deepened, and I was more convinced than ever that we had something truly special. I knew that no matter what life threw our way, we would face it together, supporting each other with the same strength and positivity that had defined our relationship from that pivotal night forward.

I couldn't dwell on this event. I needed to compartmentalise this in my brain, file and lock it away and move on. I had a new job starting on Monday and I couldn't and wouldn't let on the chaos unfolding in my personal life get in the way of my future success.

The new job at the brewery was a transformative experience for me, marking the first time I truly felt like I was embarking on a career. It wasn't just a job—it was an opportunity to build something substantial, and I embraced it wholeheartedly. I was given a company car, a Ford Falcon Station Wagon, and for events, a branded Ford F250. My first drive in the F250 was a memorable one, as I accidentally reversed into a security bollard. My boss, with his characteristic sense of humour, made a shirt commemorating the crash and presented it to me in front of everyone. It was a light-hearted moment that reminded me of the camaraderie and good-natured spirit within the company.

With a work credit card, a monthly supply of beer, and access to an onsite gym, the perks were generous, but it was the balance between road and office work that I enjoyed most. My territory started from the Coolangatta border out to Ipswich and into South Brisbane, those days were spent on the road, visiting pubs, bottle shops, and drive-throughs, ensuring stock was well-managed and venues were visually merchandised to perfection. Entertainment was a crucial part of our strategy back then. The job offered opportunities to attend events like State of Origin games, season tickets to the Gold Coast Titans, Big Day Out and other concerts and festivals, Indy 500, Doomben, Eagle Farm, Ipswich and Toowoomba race days, and Rodeos—all under the condition that our beer was on tap and readily flowing at these events. I was even tasked with weekend bar visits with two models on the Gold Coast, buying patrons our drinks. It was an era of lavish, unforgettable experiences. The brand video was set to the tune from the Arctic Monkeys' "Bet You Look Good on the Dance Floor." This track became our unofficial work anthem, energizing us and setting a high-octane tone for our outings.

A few happy memories standout in my mind. One was accidentally winning the Fashions on the Field at the Ipswich Cup, where I was asked to enter to assist in more blokes joining in but ended up winning receiving a $1,500 menswear voucher. Jimmy Barnes performed at our national conference in the Blue Mountains was another highlight. It was there that I first heard Cold Chisel's "Bow River," a song that despite being older than I, has since become a staple on any road trip playlist. Christmas parties were legendary, featuring exclusive bookings at Dreamworld where I first faced my fears of rollercoasters to show my girlfriend and workmates how brave I was, shutting my eyes for however long it took. We would embark on scavenger hunts all over Brisbane and the Coast with hilarious results.

These events, brimming with excitement and creativity, highlighted a side of corporate life that I had never witnessed or imagined in my wildest dreams. Such entertainment would likely be deemed too risky by today's standards, but at the time, it was a testament to the vibrant and dynamic work environment. I was NEVER leaving!

With every passing day, my appreciation for the role and the company grew. The experiences, budding friendships, and the opportunities made it clear to me that I was exactly where I wanted to be. I was committed to staying convinced that it was a place where I could grow, continue to thrive, and enjoy the kind of work that felt both rewarding and exhilarating. There was opportunity and I set myself a 5-year plan for where I wanted to be in the company long term.

I'd pack my DSLR camera along, documenting the incredible sights and scenes I encountered. Storm chasing in the summer was a particular thrill, capturing the dramatic weather and lightning storms that punctuated the Queensland landscape. Tony Martin and Ed Kavalee's *'Get This'* kept me laughing and entertained behind the wheel, their sharp wit and humour making the long drives more enjoyable.

I decided it was time to start this next chapter of my life under my birth name, so in 2008 flew back to Perth, Western Australia, to formally reclaim the name Isaac Curgenven. I needed to complete the process at Births, Deaths and Marriages in person. After sorting out the paperwork, I took a trip down to my hometown of Albany for the first time. The visit was a chance to reconnect with relatives and explore the landmarks tied to my family history. Driving from Perth to Albany was an adventure in itself. I didn't fully grasp the dangers of night driving in that region, where wildlife is abundant. I had several close calls with kangaroos, a red-bellied black snake, and even a massive emu (though in the moment I swore it was a cassowary). After the third narrow escape, I decided it was safer to pull over at a servo and spend the night there, driving the rest of the way in daylight.

While in Albany, I was able to spend some quality time with nan, just the two of us. It had felt like a lifetime had passed since we were together, she was much older now and in a nursing home but when I arrived, she bounced out of bed and had this newfound energy. I drove us around town, she pointed out all the historical and relevant landmarks of our lives together there in the early 80s' and she helped me dig deeper into my grandfather's service records. He had served in the Australian Imperial Force (now Australian Defence Force) working as a signaller during World War II. His service took him across Egypt, Syria, the Middle East, and the Kokoda Trail in New Guinea, as part of the 2/16th Battalion. It was a meaningful experience to uncover more about his contributions and the history of my family's involvement in such significant events. It was a stark contract to what I have been indoctrinated to believe as a kid, that his service was meaningless and he was a weak man, with a weak name.

He was awarded the following:

- 1939-45 Star

- Africa Star

- Pacific Star

- Defence Medal

- War Medal 1939-45

- Australian Service Medal 1939-45

- Australian Service Medal 1945-75 with Clasp 'SW PACIFIC'

His service in some of the most challenging and pivotal battles of the war, particularly the Kokoda Trail, a gruelling campaign marked by harsh conditions and fierce combat, underscored the resilience and courage that ran in our family. It was a reminder of the significant impact his generation had on shaping the world and preserving the freedoms we enjoy today. Unfortunately, nan admitted she had most likely thrown the medals out after pops passing, to her they were a painful memory of loss. She gifted me several pieces of her artworks during this trip and I have several of them hanging in my home still, connecting me to my past and showing my children the creative talent that runs in our DNA.

It's a source of pride to know that I come from a lineage of individuals who made significant contribution and sacrifices, and it's a reminder that my own journey is part of a much larger story.

Hillcrest

My girlfriend and I jumped in the deep end together and purchased a house on the south side of Brisbane in Hillcrest. It was a 4-bedroom lowset brick home on 900sqm that we bought for just over $300k. The plan was for this to be our long-term home, where we would start our future together. We had a pragmatic approach to the investment; if things went south, we would sell up and split it 50/50, ensuring we both left the relationship better financially than we started.

The house, however, came with an unexpected guest—a very active little spirit. We often heard the sound of running in the hallway and sometimes saw the spirit sitting with us while we watched TV. This was not just a figment of our imagination; the presence was visible, and orbs would appear on camera. We believed it was the spirit of a little girl. During renovations, we found a small stuffed bear and a box of personal belongings in the ceiling, which looked like they had been there since the 80s. We always wondered if this was her connection to the home.

Everyone has their own beliefs about the supernatural, but by this stage, I had seen, heard, and felt enough to know that spirits are real and around us every day, some as spirit guides and some seemingly tied to a place. The experience reinforced my belief in the afterlife and added a layer of mystery to our new home. Despite the eerie presence, we felt a strange comfort, as if the little girl's spirit was watching over us. It became a unique part of our story, a testament to the many unseen aspects of life that coexist with the everyday.

Wes. I have to tell you about Wes! While we were moving in, this old Ford Falcon would come flying down the street at all times throughout the day and night. Multiple times a day. We figured this dude must have been dealing drugs and looked like he was getting high off his own supply. Anyway, one day he took the corner too fast and by the time he got the car back under control it was too late, and he crashed through the wall of a lowset brick house at the end of the street. We could hear the screech of tyres and the impact of the car from the living room of our house. I walked past and saw everyone was safe and could hear other neighbours on the phone to the police. A few hours later, I went out to check again and offer any help with the police report or to arrange dinner for the family. Before I could knock on the front door, out rolled this absolute unit, covered head to toe in tattoos, asking who the hell I was and what I wanted. Quite stunned by the situation I found myself in, I explained I had saw the crash unfold and was just seeing if he needed a hand with the clean-up. I was invited in for a cup of tea and despite the crap in my pants, I tentatively went inside. There were security cameras running on a wall of TVs attached to a home security system that looked like it would rival the CIA. Large flags and weapons hung proudly on the wall. It was then that Wes introduced himself as a Sargent of Arms and explained why the police wouldn't come to his place to help. They knew who he was. I on the other hand did not, but found him a lovely bloke and was even invited around on the weekend for a BBQ. It was a refreshing reminder not to judge people by their appearance and affiliations. If you give respect, you get respect. Simple.

In the lead-up to our big move to Hillcrest, I left Simba in the care of my sister and mum at the Woodridge house. It was to be a temporary arrangement while we settled into the new place. But Simba somehow got out.

I was absolutely gutted when I found out. I burst into tears, uncontrollably, for the first time since I was a kid. I immediately sprang into action, printing posters with Simba's picture and plastering them all over the neighbourhood. I called every animal shelter I could think of, hoping someone might have taken him in. We walked the streets of Woodridge looking for him and even offered a reward, thinking that might motivate someone to help find him. But despite all my efforts, there was no sign of my little furry guy.

Simba wasn't just a pet to me; he was family. His quirky walk and playful nature brought constant joy. Losing him felt like I lost a part of myself and lost some trust with those entrusted to take care of him. Every day, I hoped for a call, a sighting, anything that would lead me back to him. Weeks turned into months, and I had to accept the harsh reality that I might never see him again. I like to think that someone found him and, seeing his deformed leg, assumed it was an injury and took him in, giving him the love and care he deserved, but I will never know.

We had our house and were gearing up to make it a true home. I'd had the ring picked out for about a year, scrimping, and saving to pay off the lay-by. My girlfriend had moved on from being a schoolteacher into the private sector as the national training and development manager for a telecommunication provider, she was the main income earner of the two of us and generously offered to buy the ring and let me give it to her. My ego was hit hard and ideals were certainly tested but I was determined to do it my way.

I had planned a grand gesture for the proposal, waiting for the perfect moment. That moment came when she was flying back from a work trip from the Northern Territory. I had told her I couldn't pick her up and would arrange a taxi instead. Meanwhile, I dressed up in a suit and flat drivers cap (to hide my identity at least a little) and took a small whiteboard to the airport. One side of the whiteboard had her name written on it, and on the other side, the big question: "Will you marry me?"

As fate would have it, she was the very last person off the plane. A crowd had gathered, curious about the suited-up weirdo with the whiteboard. The anticipation was making me sweat. Passengers and airport staff alike waited around to see what would happen. Finally, she walked through the gate, saw the whiteboard, looking puzzled at the person holding it until realizing it was me. Her eyes widened, and a smile spread across her face. I flipped the board around, knelt down, and asked the question. It was all a bit of a blur, but she said "yes".

Just after our engagement, I was cast to be on *Water Rats*, but it conflicted with a pre-booked work trip to Cairns for a launch party. Since this was a crucial career move, I knew I had to turn down the role. In hindsight, I often wonder how my life might have turned out had I taken that TV role. Up until this point, I had only ever turned down one other role in my life.

It was a tough decision, but I saw it as the right long-term move. Short term pain for long term gain. The brewery was launching new products, and I was forging important connections, so it felt like the more responsible choice at the time. Still, the what-ifs lingered.

In February 2007, I travelled north to Cairns for the event, ready to set up the venue and get everything in place for the big night. As part of the preparations, we needed to get our branded fridges up to the second level to keep the drinks cold. I was a fit young fella and had carried fridges before without a hitch. However, this time something went terribly wrong.

Only a few steps from the top of the staircase, as I was manoeuvring the fridge, I felt a sharp 'pop' in my back. With a lady from work, the venue's manager, and her daughter behind me, dropping the fridge wasn't an option. I managed to place it carefully at the top of the stairs and tried to sit down. I had played enough sports to recognise when an injury was serious, and this felt different. I struggled to hold my body weight, pushing myself up with my hands to relieve the pressure and weight from my top half.

I laid down to stretch out, hoping it was just a torn muscle, something around my hip flexor. The sensation wasn't immediately painful but felt like an unsettling nothingness with a ton of nerve pain. I don't remember much of what happened next until I was released from the Cairns hospital, everything was a bit of a blur thanks to the prescribed pain killers. I had my stuff packed up and flew back to Brisbane, I can only assume the pressure from the return leg of the flight seemed to worsen the injury. I was admitted to the hospital again in Coopers Plains, and this time the diagnosis was even graver: ruptured disks between L1, L2, L3, L4, L5, and S1.

The immediate impact was severe. I lost all feeling in my left leg from my hip/groin down to my knee. The pain made it almost impossible to sleep, sit comfortably, or drive for more than about 30 minutes, I had trouble controlling my body between the spasms and loss of sensation made even the most basic tasks difficult. The doctors delivered a sobering prognosis I would need either a spinal fusion or discectomy at the L3/L4/L5, which involved replacing the ruptured discs with new ones. However, given my age they were hesitant, the recovery was expected to be long and challenging. I was unlikely to ever play basketball again let alone lift any future children or anything heavier than 12 kilograms (about 25 pounds). To explore all possible avenues for recovery, I tried a variety of treatments: reiki massage, acupuncture, physiotherapy, chiropractic care, electro-therapy targeting the nervous system, aura cleansing, heated stone therapy, and cupping. I also explored guided steroid and cortisone injections. The prescribed drugs, like Endone and Diazepam, left me in a zombie-like state, causing me to forget weeks of my life at a time.

It was tough, both physically and mentally. I had never gone under the knife before and the thought of having back surgery at my age was scary. The surgeons explained the risks and the reality of the situation. I always prided myself on being active and fit, and the thought of not being able to do simple tasks was daunting. I was determined to stay positive, but the reality of the situation was harsh. Why oh why didn't I take the Water Rats gig instead?

I told my fiancé she should leave me. We weren't married. She didn't sign up to have a broken husband. She should cut her losses. True to form she stayed, and together we focused on my long-term recovery and planning for our wedding where we set a date for April 2008.

The Wedding

My fiancée wanted a traditional wedding with all the formalities, including a church ceremony. I was a bit hesitant, worried that the church might catch fire with me inside! After several site visits and discussions, we decided on Boulevard Gardens in Indooroopilly. It struck the right balance between formality and a relaxed, beautiful outdoor setting.

While planning the reception, I stumbled across a remarkable musician named Wiley Reed. Originally from Florida, Wiley played soulful blues piano at a small pub I worked with in Ipswich. His music was incredible, and I knew immediately that he was the perfect fit for our wedding reception. Unfortunately, Wiley fell ill in the weeks leading up to the wedding and passed away a few years later in 2012. Rest in peace, my friend. Your music touched many lives, including ours.

Mum had been on again, off again with her husband so in taking her side, I decided not to invite either of my stepfathers or their children to the wedding – except my sister of course. I didn't want anyone else exposed to the complications that had come with them. It was hard for me because I quite liked her hubby, but I had the man-to-man chat explaining the reason for the decision. Mum though couldn't understand my reasoning for not inviting my first stepfather. In her mind, he had been a significant part of our life for years, and she felt everyone should have the chance to meet him.

We ended up inviting, un-inviting and re-inviting her current husband, adding another level of stress to the planning and seating arrangements. Mum ended up moving the arrangements to suit her preference anyway. Her recurring mantra, "What about my happiness?" seemed to encapsulate her approach to the wedding.

I suggested that my little sister speak on behalf of my family, believing she could deliver a heartfelt message and we my fiancée and I trusted her with that job. Unfortunately, Mum decided to take the stage and mic herself, wearing a black cocktail dress that seemed to signal her own version of a special occasion. To cap it all off, she presented us with fluffy knitted slippers as a wedding gift and 'gifted' $500 that was originally agreed for the fridge and washing machine from our days in Woodridge. Lucky I'm not a material girl… or guy.

Nan managed to pull off a remarkable feat that no one saw coming. Even her, as by this stage of life she was losing her vision. She'd escaped from her retirement home in Albany and set off on a 4,000-kilometre journey across the country. The only problem is she didn't actually tell the home she was leaving, nor that she wasn't coming back. I know they send out Amber Alerts for missing kids, they may have raised a Purple Rinse Watch for Nan, I think when she arrived back in Brisbane and had the bulk of her family in close proximity and had the love, the support and connection again she decided to stay and see out her days with the rest of us.

Her arrival at the wedding was nothing short of a miracle and added a touch of magic to the day. Nan's adventurous spirit and determination to be there for us, despite the challenges, was a testament to her love and commitment. After the wedding, she returned to Albany briefly to wrap up her affairs, but it wasn't long before she moved back to Redcliffe to spend her remaining days closer to her daughters and wider family.

Her visit was a reminder of the deep connections, and the lengths people will go to for loved ones, even when the odds seem stacked against them. It was a heartfelt gesture that added an extra layer of significance to our special day. Nan always had my back, and my wedding day was no different.

My cousin took on the role of MC for the night, and he absolutely nailed it. He's since made quite a name for himself, becoming a regular on TV and commercials. His talent for impressions and his great sense of humour truly shone through, adding a special touch to the evening.

For our wedding song, we chose Incubus's "Dig". The lyrics, "We'll always have each other, when everything else is gone," felt like a perfect reflection of our relationship. We worked hard to save up and cover the wedding costs ourselves, with a big thank you to my in-laws who generously covered our honeymoon.

We spent a blissful week on Iririki Island Resort in Vanuatu, indulging in room service and cocktails while soaking up the beautiful surroundings. It was a perfect start to our married life, filled with relaxation and joy.

The brewery was incredibly supportive throughout the entire rehabilitation process. They provided drivers, reduced my workload, arranged for visual merchandising staff, and even covered therapy costs. They also made sure I had access to a gym and personal trainers. Despite all this support, after more than a year of rehab, it became clear that I simply couldn't continue in the job I once loved. Regrettably, I had to accept a redundancy offer in 2009.

The timing of which couldn't be worse. My wife was pregnant with our first child and had taken maternity leave from her work. While I had grown up dreaming of becoming the father that I desperately needed as a child, instead, here I was facing the prospect of unemployment. I was still struggling with my physical limitations, losing the work car and juggling mortgage payments. It was all pretty bloody daunting. It felt like I was staring down the barrel of a gun, unsure how to step up and be the husband and parent I wanted to be. For the first time in a long while, it felt like my back was firmly against the wall again, and I knew I needed to find a way to come out swinging—facing life head-on and figuring out how to make it all work.

I ended up doing short stints at 5 or 6 different jobs over a 12-month period. It felt like a constant scramble, trying to find something that would fit with my new limitations, adding to the stress the 2008 global financial crisis. Let's face it—nobody's keen to hire someone who's physically broken, but I had to find a way to keep the cash coming in.

Then came a lifeline from an old mate, who I'd worked with back at the brewery. He was now managing the local Tavern and offered me a role overseeing the drive-through and entertainment side of the business. My saint in slacks and a polo, being the legend he is, literally crafted a job around what I could physically manage and what I loved: alcohol and music.

We ran promotions through the drive-through, giving away things like TVs, eskies, and sets of golf clubs. One time, our home TV got fried by a gecko, and we were short on funds to replace it. He sorted us out by negotiating a new TV through one of his suppliers in exchange for several pallets of stock. It was up to me to clear the stock to get the TV sorted. It was a win-win, and it felt amazing to be back in a job that played to my strengths and passions. I had devised a plan to ensure the stock sold out fast.

By this stage, two major players were snapping up all the hotels and bottle shops, turning the market into a duopoly. I decided to take a stand and fired a shot across their bows with a bold newspaper advertisement.

I highlighted the range of drinks we offered that they couldn't access or price-match. It was a clear message: we had an edge. It must have pissed some people off, because shortly after, we received a letter demanding that we pull the ad. It was a testament to how effective our campaign had been—one of those moments where you know you're rattling cages. It was a small victory, but it felt like a big win for the little guy.

Speaking of little guys, the birth of our firstborn felt like a damn near miracle. We had been told early on that conceiving might be a long shot, so when my wife finally got pregnant, we were over the moon but also on edge. The pregnancy had progressed to nearly 40 weeks, and after a lot of back and forth with her obstetrician, we were pushing for a natural birth. But things didn't go as planned.

The doctors had warned us about the risks. The cervix wasn't thinning as it should, and after some tough decisions and pain management with an epidural and drugs, it became clear that a natural birth wasn't safe. We were rushed into an emergency C-section. They even had to bring in a surgeon from another hospital, a no-nonsense guy who took command of the situation.

Fear gripped me as they explained the risks. My wife was experiencing complex neurological complications and with the epidural having thinned the blood, there was a real chance one or both might not make it if there were complications. The doctor assured me if we acted now, he could save them, the room was tense, I could feel my heart pounding out of my chest as I signed the release forms, bracing for whatever might come next.

Our son was in distress, and the operation was crucial. It felt like a lifetime, but within the hour, I was holding our baby boy. The relief and joy of becoming a father were overwhelming, but so was the exhaustion and the weight of what we'd just been through.

We were both completely smitten, couldn't believe we had been gifted with a beautiful, healthy baby boy, we named him Jacob meaning 'the son of Isaac'. The three of us spent the next week at Sunnybank Hospital, navigating the whirlwind of recovery and slowly stepping into parenthood. Like every other dad in the place, I had fitted and refitted the baby seat several times to ensure it was safe, secure and locked in place. I felt this overwhelming sense of achievement and satisfaction with life, that by twenty-five I was married, had a son, owned a home, and had a fun job. I had played basketball in the USA and seen my face on the big screen. Those childhood goals I had dreamed of had come true.

Excitedly we returned home to Hillcrest to find there was a letter on the doorstep from my mum - assuming it was a congratulatory message – we opened it together to read she was seeking grandparental guardianship of our newborn son.

Think about that for a minute.

It was at that point I drew a line in the sand. I sought legal counsel, and my solicitor advised me the decision had to be made to cut off all contact and access. After everything we had been through, I realised that continuing the same patterns wasn't just unhealthy—it was unsustainable. The decision to cut my mum out of my life wasn't made lightly, but it became clear that it was necessary to protect the life and family we were trying to build together.

The constant interference, the volatile dynamics, and the emotional toll were simply too much. I needed to prioritise the well-being of my family over any lingering sense of obligation or hope that things might change. It wasn't about holding grudges or forgetting the past—it was about recognising that the relationship had become a source of harm rather than support.

Making the decision was heart-wrenching. I grappled with

feelings of guilt and fear of being misunderstood. Mum had been my everything during my early life, but I knew that for our future to thrive, boundaries had to be set, and sometimes that meant making the toughest choices.

As such, I made the decision to step back and cut off contact. Disconnected the home phone, changed mobile numbers, set up new email accounts, our mailbox was bombarded with letters that would range from angry, to sad and everything in between. In one she questioned if she should have listened to all those people twenty-something years ago and had the abortion – of me – followed by several letters simply saying sorry repeated dozens of times on the page. In the end, it was my only choice. And it's a choice I still live with today.

The journey wasn't easy, and the decision to cut ties with my mum was one of the hardest things I've ever done. But it was necessary. For my family, for our peace, and for the future we wanted to build. In the end, we are the sum of our experiences, and I wouldn't change mine for anything. They made me who I am today—a husband, a father, a man determined to break the cycle and build a better future.

Since then I have been blessed with another two beautiful and healthy children; Hope (after my wife's maiden name) who was born in 2011 and our youngest Theodore (named by his siblings) completing our family in 2015. I like to think we have the best times together and while maintaining a distinction between father and friend have a healthy and happy relationship. They mean the world to me and each one holds a special place in my heart and tattooed across my chest.

Life is about learning, growing, and making choices that align with our values. It's about surrounding ourselves with people who lift us up and letting go of those who bring us down. It's about living authentically and embracing the journey, knowing that every step, no matter how difficult, is a step towards the life we want to create and be proud of. Set your goals and chase em.

Saying Goodbye.

My life feels full of goodbyes.

Firstly, Simba. I'll never love another pet the way I loved you.

The Curgenven name traces back to Cornwall, England, in the 18th century and I feel a strong responsibility to honour its legacy.

After some years of searching, I found pop's burial site in 2007. It took the groundskeeper some time to locate the unmarked grave, eighteen years since his passing seemingly lost in the records of time, a war hero from the 2/16th. There were no flowers or keepsakes marking his resting place, pop deserved better than that, I spent hours there reconnecting with his spirit. I had sought contact with him several times and received signs that he was watching over me. I wish I had the words to explain how much pop meant to me and how incensed I was to find his unmarked grave, the lack of love, respect, and appreciation for someone who served his country was a loving husband, father, and grandpa. I filed an application to pay for a headstone, however, it was denied as I wasn't the power of attorney on the estate. When my request was raised again, it was rejected. In the years that followed, nothing had been done so I did it my own way. I have his dog tags tattooed around my neck, a poppy flower and a cross on my arm to always have him with me. If no one else saw the need to have a permanent mark for his legacy, I sure as hell did.

Nan and I had some great years together, though our time was sporadic: from 1983 to 1984, 1988 to 1993, and again from 2009 to 2014 until she passed at Redcliffe. Knowing that she wouldn't be around forever, I created a book for her to document her stories, memories, recipes, and photos—a beautiful keepsake that I will treasure forever. Her artwork still hangs proudly in my home and I still have the letters we exchanged, but I deeply regret not having a recording of her voice recounting the stories of "Arna" as the sound of her voice is fading from my memory.

Growing up their home at 'The Pines' in Burpengary had a communal tennis court where we played together. There was also a tyre swing hanging from an old pine tree. But what I loved most was playing kickball at the end of the cul-de-sac. When the ball would go over the edge, Pop would venture down into the ravine to retrieve it. Driving past as an adult the smell of the area transports me back to those joyful times, and I roll down my windows, breathing deeply, in hopes of rekindling those cherished memories. All relationships eventually come to an end, and you're always left wishing for more time. Nan was in Redcliffe while I was on the Gold Coast—only a 90-minute drive away. I wish I had made the trip more often. We saw each other about once every month or two, and she met my first two children. She was absolutely smitten with them. It's easy to let work, family and life responsibilities get in the way, but I implore you to make the time for those people who you truly love.

My saddest memory was choosing to say goodbye at the funeral home. I sat with her body, talking about memories and my family, filling her in on the latest news and promised I would see her again one day. I touched her one last time, hoping to feel that familiar soft skin. But she was cold, and no longer the snuggly, warm nan I remembered. My lasting memory is of our last visit together, I showed her how to take a selfie while we were laughing and talking about my upcoming trip to the USA, but instead, I was left with this final, long goodbye.

At the service, I did my best to hold it together, but when I carried her out, the tears flowed uncontrollably. I stayed there for hours afterward, unable to bring myself to the wake. It seemed everyone was too eager to move on and start sorting through her belongings. Instead, I chose to visit Pop, who is laid to rest at Redcliffe, and spent some quiet time with him, just being in the moment.

I know Nan wanted to protect me from my stepfather, but she didn't quite know how. As long as Mum stayed, there was little she could do. Nan saw through his façade; after all, her gift in art was capturing the true essence of her subjects. I imagine she saw straight through him, recognizing his manipulations. With Mum being isolated and set against her, the rift in their relationship only widened. Mum confided in my stepfather about her past, and he used that information to undermine their relationship and keep them apart.

My stepfather always hinted at a secret he would reveal on his deathbed, claiming it was something we'd all want to stick around to discover. Mum had speculated that it was an unsolved murder in North Queensland, but in 2023 his time came to an end, there was no dramatic announcement or revelation. Despite all his plans for financial freedom he didn't leave much behind for his biological children. In researching and writing these stories, I've tried to piece together what I can about him. However, my searches have turned up more questions than answers. The only records I could find online was for the name we knew him as were for a man who passed away in 1933, four years before his birth year and his death certificate didn't add any insight to his parents, siblings, past marital status or anything else of use to trace his history. Anyway, that's his story—fragmented and elusive. It's no longer my concern. I hope he has found the peace and prosperity he sought in the afterlife. As for me, I'm moving forward, focusing on the present and the future.

Cutting Mum out of my life felt like a death. My mum was the most beautiful woman in the world in my eyes growing up, her cooking, hugs and belief in me were unwavering. She had a smile that was a mirror image of my own, our side profiles were almost identical. She was a softly spoken, natural hippie, with a creative spirit that shone through in everything she did—writing songs, crafting lyrics, and spinning stories. She was a fantastic cook, and her culinary skills were a source of joy in our home. We spent countless hours together in the kitchen, where I would experiment with my own recipes. My school lunches were the stuff of legend; her sandwiches were so coveted that she always had to pack an extra one. Our relationship was deeply affectionate. I cherished the moments I could rest my head in her lap while she ran her fingers through my hair. It was as if she counted each strand with the tenderness of her touch, offering a soothing calm that I always looked forward to. We were emotionally connected on a profound level—when she was upset, I would feel her emotions and reflect them as if we were one. I never outgrew Mum's cuddles and was never embarrassed to be seen with her.

As a kid, as long as I was near Mum, I was content. She was my safety blanket, my anchor in a world that often felt uncertain. I would become inconsolable whenever she left me at daycare or with a babysitter; the thought of being separated from her terrified me. Our time together was filled with adventure and creativity. We travelled, went to the movies, explored beaches, played in the park, built train sets, cooked together, read stories, and dabbled in art.

In those early days, mum was a smoker, and I loathed the smell. I would secretly hide her cigarette packs in the bucket seats of her old Ford to keep them away from her. In her later letters, Mum expressed doubts about her ability to raise me on her own, questioning her capacity to provide the discipline and guidance I needed. Reflecting now, I realize these doubts were likely the result of my stepfather's manipulation. Mum would have shared her deepest thoughts and vulnerabilities with him, only for them to be exploited and used to control her. For much of my childhood, Mum was a stay-at-home parent. She would handle the school run, and we were always excited to see her in the afternoon when we returned. Mum was the one who drove me to sports and cheered from the stands, her support making those moments feel like they were all about me.

But underneath the surface, there were deep-seated feelings of abandonment. It often seemed like Mum's desire for freedom took precedence over what was best for me. Reflecting on the move from WA to QLD felt like a choice that placed her needs above mine. The same went for her relationship with my stepfather, who was physically and mentally abusive. Despite knowing how much I despised him, Mum stayed with him, and his presence caused me tremendous distress from a young age. Then when our family unit split in 2001, Mum's quest for independence led her to move to Newcastle, but she did so without me. There was no offer for me to move with her; she simply assumed I would move in with my girlfriend and her family. When Mum eventually settled down with her husband, the volatility of their relationship caused issues at my wedding and worst of all when I came home to find the note on my doorstep seeking a shared custody arrangement. Once again, it seemed to be all about her happiness, with little regard for the impact on me or the stability of our family.

I am not a mum, and I never will be, so I approach this next part with the utmost love and respect, acknowledging that I can't fully grasp what it was like for her. However, as we grew older, it increasingly seemed that Mum's longing for happiness took precedence over everything else. From Mum's perspective, I was the one man who was always there for her, sticking by her through thick and thin. But I had to prioritize my own well-being and the stability of my marriage over the ongoing dynamics that threatened to undermine both. I couldn't be married to my mum and my wife.

She now goes by various names, her shifting identities seemed to reflect the turmoil within. She would say, "A daughter is a daughter for life, a son is a son until he takes a wife," which always felt deeply unfair to me. It wasn't my marriage that tore us apart, but her refusal to accept it.

The decision to distance myself from Mum was one of the hardest choices I've ever had to make. It's a decision weighed down with the gravity of countless memories and the enduring ache of what could have been. Mum was the constant in my life, the first face I'd see in the morning and the last at night. She was there to tuck me into bed, kiss me on the forehead, and stroke my hair to soothe me into sleep. She was the heartbeat of my daily life, a reassuring presence amidst the chaos and change. As I reflect on our relationship, it's both heart-wrenching and necessary to acknowledge the distance I've had to create. I can't recall a distinct smell or a singular first memory that defines her in my mind. Instead, it's the countless, everyday moments that stand out—the way she made me feel safe and loved, the way she was my anchor in a world that was often uncertain.

Yet, as much as I yearned for those comforting rituals, I had to recognize that the patterns of our relationship were no longer serving either of us well. Despite the pain of setting boundaries and the heartache of distance, it was necessary to safeguard my own well-being and that of my family. The memories of her kisses and calming touches now serve as bittersweet reminders of the love we once shared and the painful necessity of my decision.

Ending this book is not about erasing the past but rather about acknowledging the complexity of the relationship and the steps I had to take to build a healthier future. It is about finding peace within myself and creating a space where I can cherish the positive aspects of our shared history while moving forward with clarity and strength. I'm challenging the rules of the 'big people's game' and focusing more on educating with love, knowledge and laughter instead of fear, violence and control. Reflecting back isn't about placing blame, instead seeking better outcomes.

The road hasn't been easy, and the echoes of those everyday moments still resonate within me. But I've learned that sometimes, even the most cherished relationships require boundaries to preserve the love and respect that once existed. And while the pain of that decision will always linger, it is a testament to the resilience and growth that have come from navigating this difficult journey.

As Johnny Cash said in the song Hurt, "everyone I know goes away in the end".

Saying Goodbye.

Dear Kids,

It's been one heck of a journey writing this all out, warts and all for you to read and uncover. My hope is you learn from my mistakes and avoid having to go through those yourself. I am sharing this with you in full transparency and honesty as this wasn't something readily available to me as a child. I refuse to be defined solely by the events of my life. I wanted counselling to fix me, just de-program the years of chaos, but instead, taught me that I am the sum of all my parts, each one contributing to the person I am today. Without those moments, both good and bad, I wouldn't have the perspective or resilience that shapes my decisions now. I love my life and what we have created together so even if given the chance, I wouldn't change a thing.

It's taken a lot of personal work, reflection, and determination to carve out a new path. I've strived to become the man, father, and husband I want to be, rather than repeating the patterns I witnessed growing up. That journey hasn't been easy, but it's been essential for my growth and the well-being of my family. I will never hide the truth from you nor withhold information that you deem important, this wasn't something provided to or readily available to me when I was younger so I understand how important it can be.

In my view, the whole purpose of raising a family is to ensure that each generation can be better than the last. This means learning from past mistakes, building on successes, and fostering an environment where growth and improvement are not just encouraged but expected. It's about creating a legacy where our children don't have to endure the same struggles, and instead, they can build upon the foundation we lay for them.

I firmly hold the belief, "if you love something, set it free. If it comes back, it's meant to be." I understand all too well that I cannot control someone's pace of change any more than I can control the wind from blowing. Who I was at fifteen, twenty-five, and thirty-five are three very different people. As a result, my circle of friends and family has changed significantly, and that's okay.

All I hope is that your mum and I change at a similar pace and in a similar direction. The reality is, if we don't and we drift apart, she will always hold that special place in my heart as the mother of my children. I've never felt a love as strong as when I watched her go through the gruelling experience that is childbirth. Every year, we do a check-in to understand where we are as individuals, as a couple, and as a family, and what goals we are setting for ourselves in the upcoming year, it's a true partnership built on the foundation of friendship.

There have been a few times where we gave ourselves six months to work on correcting the direction we were heading. True to this fundamental belief of freedom in a relationship, "I won't fight you, but I will fight for you." This approach acknowledges that while we can't control the natural evolution of each other's paths, we can commit to understanding, supporting, and nurturing our relationship through open communication and mutual respect.

Navigating the complexities of change and growth within a relationship requires patience, empathy, and a willingness to adapt. It means recognizing that people evolve, and sometimes that evolution can lead to different places. However, by staying connected and checking in regularly, we create opportunities to realign and reinforce our bond, ensuring that even if we change, we do so together, or at least with understanding and respect for each other's journeys.

The "Five Languages of Love" is a fantastic book to better understand how to connect with your partner. It's a real revelation that just because something is what you would want, it doesn't mean it's the same for your partner. We all have different ways we express and receive love, and this book helps bridge that gap. A good friend recommended it to me, and it has been invaluable in deepening the connection with my partner.

There are two types of friends in this life – LTF and GTF. Let me explain; long-time friendships (LTF) are essential, they provide continuity and support, helping you stay grounded amidst life's changes. They remind us of our roots and the journey we've been on and our 'past lives'. They offer a unique perspective and a sense of history that newer relationships don't have. They are the ones who offer a shoulder to cry on, provide support when chips are down, and celebrate your successes with genuine happiness. These are your real ones.

Don't get them confused for good-time friends (GTF) who add fun and excitement to your life but not much depth. They're great for spontaneous outings, lively parties, and creating memorable moments. However, they might not always be around when the going gets tough. It's important not to over-invest in GTFs at the expense of LTFs. Enjoy their company but remember where to place your priorities.

The saying, "Blood may be thicker than water," holds some truth, but it's also essential to remember that you can't survive without water. In this analogy, water represents those friends who sustain you, nourish your spirit, and keep you grounded. Blood, representing family, is crucial too, but sometimes, family ties can become toxic. Just as water can go bad, so can relationships, whether with family or friends. Your godmother is the prime example of this in your lives. You are all incredibly lucky to have someone like that by your side. I had an auntie like her growing up and proved invaluable for me getting through this life.

Trust your gut; your instincts are often your best guide. We all make mistakes, but they are essential for growth. Learn from them, let go of the guilt, and move forward with the wisdom gained. Reconnect with nature whenever you can. There's a unique peace in the great outdoors that you won't find anywhere else. Whether it's a hike in the bush, a swim in the ocean, or just a walk in the park, nature has a way of grounding you. Simple acts of kindness can make a world of difference in someone's day and enrich your own life.

For personal growth, travel will be your best learning and experience. It broadens your horizons, exposes you to new cultures, and challenges your perceptions. Whether you're trekking through the outback, exploring bustling cities, or relaxing on a remote beach, each journey will teach you something invaluable about the world and yourself.

Do things that scare you. The sense of achievement you'll feel will remind you that you're more capable than you think. Whether it's skydiving, public speaking, or starting a new career, pushing your boundaries will build your confidence and resilience. You can always make more money, but you can't make more time. Prioritize experiences over material possessions. Find a partner who shares your values, and you'll have a lifelong companion in both fun and friendship.

It's easy to get caught up in the demands of work but make sure you switch off when you get home, take time for yourself, and ensure your loved ones know by your actions and not simply your words that they come first.

Boys, it's okay to cry. Emotions are not a sign of weakness but a part of being human. Don't try to fit into anyone else's perception of what a 'man' should be. Authenticity is your greatest strength. You'll do just fine.

This is starting to sound like that "Everybody's Free (To Wear Sunscreen)," but these lessons are timeless.

Most importantly, don't take life too seriously. It's not about making it through unscathed but about enjoying the ride. Life is an unpredictable adventure filled with highs and lows, embrace the ride with a sense of humour and a positive outlook. If you lived to the ripe old age of 90, you would have just under 33,000 days on this Earth. None of us are going to make it out alive anyway, so you might as well have some fun along the way.

All my love,
Dad

Dear Kids,

Author bio:

The Big People's Game is the debut creative non-fiction story detailing Isaac's personal journey, experiences, and learnings through life.

Isaac shares his story with honesty and transparency, aiming to leave a legacy that highlights his personal and family history for future generations. He firmly believes that by sharing our individual journeys, we discover common threads that connect us all.

Isaac is passionate about challenging the stereotype that children who witness domestic and family violence inevitably follow in those footsteps. He is living proof that breaking the cycle is not only possible, but achievable through hard work and sacrifice. His mission is to inspire others and ensure that each generation can build on the progress of the last, rising above trauma and creating a better future.

One of Isaac's proudest career achievements has been the creation of the 'Magnolia Place' concept—an initiative that connects charity partners within shopping centres. Over the past few years, this concept has positively impacted thousands of lives by bringing essential services to where people naturally gather. Isaac's goal is to continue expanding this initiative across Australia, ensuring vital support is available to those who need it most.

Alongside his professional accomplishments, Isaac is committed

Author bio:

to sharing his personal journey in a way that helps others uncover the mindset required to overcome life's challenges. While he doesn't claim to have all the answers, his lived experience allows him to speak with raw honesty and humour to audiences of all ages. His aim is to offer insights into resilience, showing that, no matter the adversity, it is possible to rise above it and thrive.

Follow along as the journey continues to unfold via – isaac.curgenven.speaker on Instagram

To book for speaking engagements please contact on email – isaac.curgenven@live.com.au

Spotify Playlist – scan the QR code below, sit back and enjoy 😊

www.ingramcontent.com/pod-product-compliance
Lightning Source LLC
Chambersburg PA
CBHW062037290426
44109CB00026B/2646